Bavel

Bavel

Modern Recipes Inspired
by the Middle East

Ori Menashe &
Genevieve Gergis
with Lesley Suter

Photographs by
Nicole Franzen

TEN SPEED PRESS
California | New York

Contents

What Is Bavel?

Bavel (pronounced bah-VELLE) is the Hebrew name for Babel, the setting for the biblical story of the Tower of Babel. The myth seeks to explain the creation of all human languages, but over time it has evolved, for many, to become a metaphor for the myriad of cultural, spiritual, and political differences that divide us. To us, the term "Bavel" represents a world—and more specifically, a Middle East—*before* this separation, before all of the fraught man-made borders and conflicting beliefs that have come to define the region today.

This unified version of the Middle East is alive and well in its food, where you can still taste the traces of shared culinary traditions. Like the land itself, these cuisines have, over time, become divided, labeled, and claimed. But at their core, these are the intertwined flavors of a communal past. This is what we aim to celebrate at Bavel, the freedom to cook things that we love without loyalty to any specific country. This is cooking without borders.

Bavel is a restaurant of family and heritage; it's an ode to the food we grew up eating and the food we love to eat today. It is a restaurant that applies the techniques we've learned to the flavors we inherited. And we're honored to share them with you—every night at our restaurant and now here, in the pages of this book.

Our Story

"Bestia is something we learned how to do; Bavel is something we were born into."

I couldn't help myself. We had just opened our first restaurant, Bestia, in downtown L.A.'s arts district; Genevieve was pregnant with our first daughter, Saffron; but still, the idea for a second restaurant wouldn't leave. It began as a craving. After opening an Italian restaurant and working my way through Italian kitchens for a decade before that, I found that I craved something different when cooking for myself. I craved the flavors of home—shawarma, shakshuka, falafel, tahini. So, I began making these dishes on my days off—the foods of my father and my grandmother; the foods of my childhood in Israel, as well as my family's roots in Georgia, Morocco, Persia, and beyond. These dishes struck a chord with Genevieve, too. Her father had emigrated from Egypt as a college student, and she felt a tug of nostalgia as she tasted the almost-forgotten spices of her youth.

Then I started scribbling down recipes. Just fragments at first—an aroma, a flavor, or a sensation I wanted to capture. During our first vacation after opening Bestia, Genevieve remembers waking up every morning to find me hunched over my notebook, writing. Eventually, what began as a collection of loose ideas developed into Bavel—a restaurant (and now a cookbook) that takes the techniques and experiences we've learned throughout our professional lives and applies them to the flavors of the Middle East.

Normally, Genevieve would have been the first to say no. We had a kid on the way and a busy restaurant to run. But she, too, felt that this was the right next move. Since opening Bestia, we'd been offered the opportunity to open other branches elsewhere. But Bestia is not something that can be reproduced. It is unique, and of a place, and it would have felt unnatural to try to duplicate it. The idea for Bavel was different, though; like a new sibling—connected but apart. It was a concept that spoke to our shared heritage while taking inspiration from our work, our lives, our travels, and our city. This we knew we could do.

It was 2013, and the modern obsession with Middle Eastern food had yet to really resonate in the United States. In L.A., the food of Israel, Palestine, Lebanon, and Armenia was still largely relegated to the world of fast food, banquet cooking, and the broader genre of "immigrant cuisine," which carries with it certain false assumptions of ambition, quality, and cost. Genevieve and I wanted to do something different. We wanted to showcase how complex these flavors can be, how the deft use of spices and fire can create something ten times as powerful as any French sauce. And it was very important to Genevieve that

we do this in a space that didn't feel like some lantern-lit set from *The Arabian Nights*, but in a modern, airy place that matched its L.A. surroundings and channeled the sun-bleached palette of a Mediterranean beach town.

But if the opening of Bestia had been intimidating, this venture was even more so. I'd spent years honing my style of Italian cooking, but the food of my upbringing was another story. I had eaten shawarma and pita a thousand times, but I'd never made them myself. So, I had to go back—before my time as a chef, before I ever even thought about cooking professionally. I had to think back to my family's home kitchen in Israel where I had watched my father, the greatest cook I have ever known, whip thick tahini into an ethereal spread, hang sheets of fish roe to dry in the sun for bottarga, and knead loaf after loaf of whole-grain bread. I thought back to the years of post–soccer game shawarma runs, trips to the market for Jerusalem mixed-grill sandwiches, and long café lunches, spent swiping fresh-baked pita through piles of hummus.

Genevieve, too, looked to sense memory for inspiration. She'd only ever worked as a professional pastry chef at Bestia, but growing up in Southern California, she remembered the trays of shredded phyllo soaked in floral honey syrup that would appear after large family feasts—and how even though she'd say she didn't like it, she would sneak second and third bites when nobody was watching. She remembered how after years of complaining about the lack of chocolate chip cookies and snickerdoodles in the house, the fragrant desserts of her father's homeland had stopped, and how as an adult, she had begged for their reappearance.

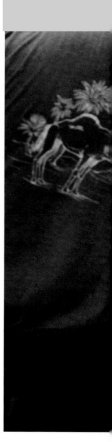

But while the flavors of our past helped inspire us, we didn't want this to be a menu of re-creations—of traditional Middle Eastern food or my grandmother's food or my dad's food. We wanted it to be something unique and to prove to ourselves that we could cook our own food, completely. (The only exception is my hummus, which is directly inspired by the version served at the legendary Abu Hassan in Jaffa, the ancient port city in Tel Aviv. Because once you've had the best hummus in the world, you can't think of anything else.)

With our concept in place, then came the waiting. First one space fell through, then another. It took almost three years before we were even able to begin construction, and during that time, a number of high-profile Middle Eastern restaurants began to emerge on the American food scene. A national interest in so-called "Mediterranean" flavors began to take hold, za'atar and labneh became more and more commonplace, and restaurants serving fancy falafel opened across L.A. All the while, Bavel was percolating; even as we worked on the cookbook for Bestia, we were honing Bavel's recipes, obsessing over ingredients, perfecting the bar program, and finalizing the decor.

By the time we finally opened the doors to Bavel in a former iron-ore plant near the banks of the Los Angeles River in 2018, it didn't feel—to us anyway—much like a new restaurant. It felt like a piece of us we'd lived with for years and, in a sense, for our entire lives. And since that moment, beneath a chandelier of vines, I, Genevieve, and our incredible team of cooks, waiters, hostesses, bartenders, and staff have worked continuously to bring our original dream to life—a restaurant and a menu that feels at once new and familiar, with flavorful echoes of the Middle East and a spirit that is wholeheartedly L.A.

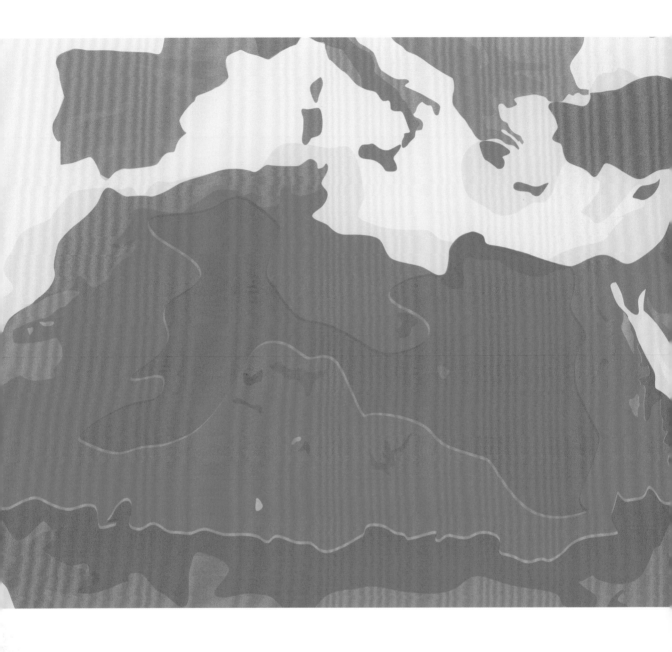

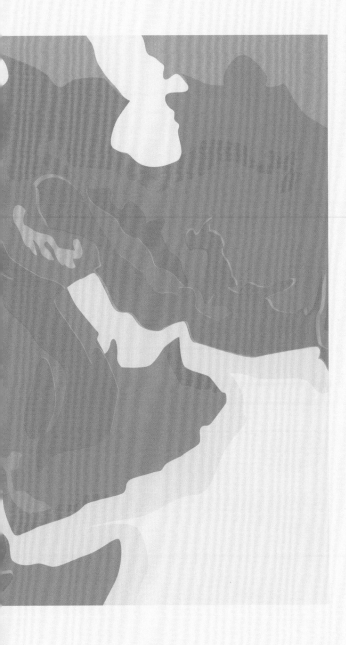

The Middle East

There is no region on earth whose map is more in flux than the strip of land between India and the Mediterranean. Borders are constantly shifting and with them, country names and political alliances. While the foods of Bavel are not meant to channel any specific country's cuisine—and certainly not any political or spiritual beliefs—there are recipes and ingredients in this book where we do mention a possible place of origin, as we have learned them from our ancestors, our travels, or our studies. We do this out of respect for the food's history but not out of loyalty to any particular land at present.

About This Book

The recipes in this book take the mission of our restaurant one step further into the realm of the personal, incorporating traditional family recipes and favorites we cook at home into our repertoire of Middle Eastern dishes. In that spirit, several of the techniques and ingredients have been altered slightly from the versions we serve at Bavel to account for everyone's varying access to ingredients and equipment. Even at the restaurant, we shift recipes depending on the season, and our adaptations here are designed to preserve the flavor and quality of each dish. But wherever possible, we have maintained the integrity of the original dishes; if a recipe seems a little challenging, the reward is worth it.

Weights and Measures

A handful of the recipes in this book feature both volume measures and metric weight measurements. This isn't to appear fancy or to annoy the hell out of our publishers. This is because for certain recipes, like breads, accuracy is critical for consistent results, and measuring ingredients (using a kitchen scale) is inarguably more precise—*and, in many cases, easier*—than cooking with cups, teaspoons, and tablespoons. We are also aware, however, that not everyone has a kitchen scale, and most recipes will turn out just fine when measured by volume; that is why we always provide a volume measure even if we recommend by weight. Still, weighing rather than scooping (at the very least, while baking) is a practice worth learning. Your dishwasher will thank you.

Ingredients

Some recipes in this book feature ingredients that may be more readily available in some areas of the country than others, including certain chiles, herbs, and spices. While we offer substitutions for some specialty ingredients, it's now possible to find a Middle Eastern market in almost every city in the United States. Visit one near you, explore the aisles, and meet your neighbors. Additionally, many ingredients are now available from online retailers, including Amazon and igourmet. Also, all recipes call for kosher salt unless otherwise specified. We use Diamond brand kosher salt, which will give you the most accurate results.

Chapter 1

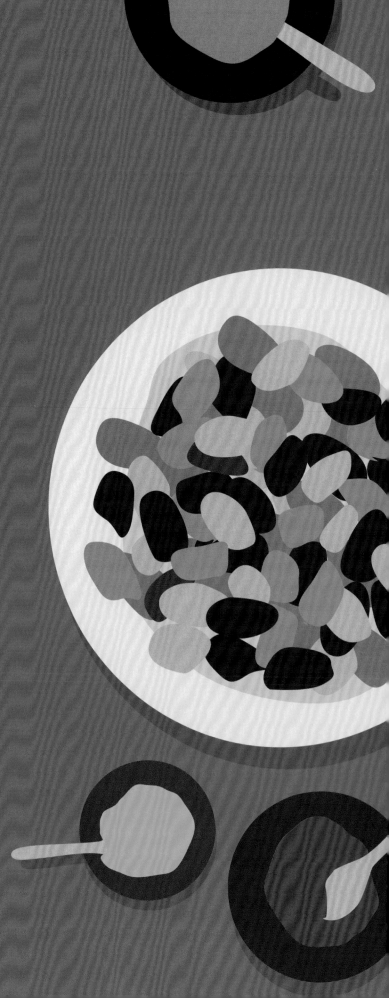

Pantry

Middle Eastern food is, at its core, about the layering of flavors—spices, acids, pickles—to create something powerful out of what are often very simple raw ingredients.

I sometimes say that Italian food is like cheating. Sure, you can incorporate all sorts of complex flavor amplifiers and umami boosters—and we do that at Bestia—but you could also just throw some burrata and prosciutto on a plate, and it would be delicious. Middle Eastern food is different. That sense of luxury and craveability has to be coaxed out of the food by blooming spices, mixing citrus and vinegars, grilling, smoking, and adding final pops of toasted seeds and fresh herbs.

The spice blends, pickles, sauces, and stocks in this chapter form the building blocks of our version of Middle Eastern flavor. They are the bold foundations from which we start each dish and the elegant flourishes with which we finish them. The dips and spreads included here are themselves enough to base a meal around—some warm pita swiped through a plate of baba ghanoush, hummus, or tahini can be a mind-blowing lunch in itself. At home, all of these staples are endlessly versatile and can be used to add complexity to recipes beyond those contained in this book. Put some pickled turnips in a salad, serve spicy zhoug with grilled chicken, or sprinkle dukkah over flatbread. Once you put the time and effort into building an excellent pantry, the rest will come easily.

Spices

If I close my eyes, I can still smell the spice markets of my youth, the intense aroma of chiles, seeds, pods, and powders from throughout the region, colliding in cramped alleyways. Growing up, my dad would often take me with him on trips to the market, where I would see dozens and dozens of stalls selling spices along with pantry items like pickles, olives, dried fish, and preserved lemons. The smell of it all together was irresistible—like wafts of pure hunger. After the smell came the color, vibrant hues of reds, oranges, blacks, and all the shades in between. It's the color, my dad taught me, that hints at the quality. The more vibrant looking the spices are, the fresher they taste. Eventually, we'd walk out with a few bags of this and that, clothes smelling of saffron and ginger, and stop for a shawarma or falafel—before heading home.

Cooking with spices is a technique you have to learn, and it's vastly different from the way you manipulate flavor in other styles of cooking. For instance, Italian cuisine uses salt and umami to drive flavor, but too much salt can enhance some spices to the point of being overwhelming. Instead, Middle Eastern cooking—much like Indian cooking—builds flavor by adding spices in stages throughout the cooking process. In the end, even without umami-rich ingredients like fish sauce or anchovies or cheese, the taste is addictive. It's the layers of spice that keep your palate wanting more. That is what we try to do with spices at Bavel. We layer our dishes with notes of dry spices, fresh spices, and herbs, and in the end, each bite is a roller coaster, something utterly craveable.

Toasting, Grinding, and Storing

Almost all spices should be toasted before using; the heat helps to release their distinct oils and aroma.

To toast whole spices:

Add the spices to a small skillet and toast over very low heat for about 3 minutes, tossing occasionally to prevent burning, until fragrant but not smoking, warm but not hot. Spread out the spices on a sheet pan and let cool. If grinding, let cool completely first.

To toast sesame seeds:

The oils in sesame seeds can burn easily, so the seeds need to be toasted more gently. In a small skillet over low heat, lightly toast the whole sesame seeds for about 1 minute, constantly stirring with a spatula, until fragrant and warm throughout to the touch. You can toast up to 2 days before using; cool and store in an airtight container at room temperature.

To grind whole spices:

Most recipes in this book are fine with store-bought preground spices. For some, like cumin, coriander, and mustard seed, we prefer to grind them ourselves, using either an electric spice grinder or a mortar and pestle. When grinding yourself, start with at least ½ cup of whole spices—much less and they won't grind correctly—and measure the amounts for each recipe from the final yield.

Green cardamom is true cardamom and is the variety you'll find marked as just cardamom at the store. We grind ours with the husk to mellow it a little bit. If you're grinding your own, grind it whole with the husk in a spice grinder.

To store spices:

Spices lose their flavor over time, so freshness is key. Untoasted spices can be kept in an airtight container for up to 6 months, toasted spices for 2 to 3 weeks.

The Bavel Spice Rack

These spices and aromatics are the building blocks of flavor at Bavel and for many of the recipes in this book. Some are used on their own; others go into blends that become new spices unto themselves. Here is a list of what you'll find on the shelves in the Bavel pantry and each spice's flavor profile.

Aleppo Pepper—*fruity with mild cumin flavor, moderate heat*

Allspice—*strong, spicy taste that is sweetly pungent with peppery overtones*

Borage Flowers—*fresh vegetal taste, similar to cucumber, with a light sweetness*

Caraway Seed—*mild licorice flavor; earthy with a little pepper and citrus*

Black Cardamom—*herbaceous warming spice with notes of menthol*

Green Cardamom—*flavors of citrus, mint, and slightly spicy*

Chile de Árbol—*grassy and nutty flavor with a searing, acidic heat*

Chile Flakes—*crushed chile peppers; mildly sweet with moderate heat*

Cinnamon—*made from bark; a sweet and woodsy warming spice that can also be earthy*

Cloves—*strong and sweet warming spice with a bitter, astringent flavor*

Coriander Seed—*dried cilantro seeds; a warm spice with hints of citrus and nuttiness*

Cumin Seed—*earthy, nutty, and spicy taste with bitter, warm lemon undertones*

Fennel Pollen—*strong, sweet flavor of licorice with hints of honey and citrus*

Fennel Seed—*warm and sweet with hints of licorice*

Fenugreek Seed—*sweet and nutty with strong notes of maple; can be bitter*

Black Garlic—*specially aged garlic that is sweet and earthy with a sticky datelike texture*

Ground Ginger—*warm, spicy bite that is slightly sweet and more subtle than fresh ginger*

Guajillo Pepper—*mild, sweet heat with hints of pine, tart berries, and smoky notes*

Juniper Berry—*tart and sharp with a piney flavor*

Kashmiri Pepper—*mild heat and full flavor; vibrant red coloring*

Licorice Powder—*sweet and reminiscent of fennel and anise*

Black Lime—*dried, almost completely dehydrated lime with a sweet yet tangy citrus flavor*

Marash Pepper—*Turkish pepper with fruity and earthy undertones and a mild heat*

Marigold—*bitter and slightly spicy; peppery*

Morita Chile—*smoked red jalapeños that taste fruity and slightly acidic with hints of smoke*

Mustard Seed—*sharp and pungent, slightly spicy*

Nigella Seed—*herbaceous, slightly bitter with a warm onion flavor*

Nutmeg—*nutty, slightly sweet, and warm*

Dried Orange Peel—*sweet, sharp, and tangy with hints of bitterness*

Paprika—*sweet, slightly fruity with a very mild heat*

Black Peppercorn—*sharp and pungent; earthiness with woody and piney tones*

Pink Peppercorn—*sweet, fruity flavor with a peppery bite*

Puya Pepper—*pungent, intense heat with fruity flavors and licorice notes*

Rose Petals—*very aromatic floral sweetness and sometimes tart*

Saffron—*subtly sweet and floral aroma with a light honey flavor*

White Sesame—*just the kernel of the seed with a sweet and nutty flavor*

Black Sesame—*contains hull and kernel of the seed; slightly bitter and nutty*

Star Anise—*sweet and spicy, similar to licorice*

Sumac—*wild sour berry with a tart almost lemony flavor*

Cured Sumac—*sumac packed in salt to preserve, with a bright sour, slightly fermented flavor*

Turmeric—*in the ginger family; earthy and bitter in flavor*

Urfa Pepper—*Turkish chile pepper; smoky and sweet raisinlike taste*

Za'atars

Za'atar is a strong, oregano-like herb that grows wild throughout different parts of the Middle East. It's also the key ingredient for the favorite Middle Eastern seasoning of the same name, a flavorful mixture of herbs, sesame seeds, and sumac that's dusted over fresh flatbread to add texture and depth or stirred into olive oil for dipping. Za'atar doesn't grow in L.A., so instead, I use a blend of marjoram, thyme, and sumac to get a similar flavor, as well as a little sugar for balance and some citric acid to help the sumac pop.

At Bavel, we make a number of different za'atar blends, using rose petals, dried mushrooms, or even fig leaves to bring out certain characteristics. The rose version is floral and herbaceous and holds up well to luxurious, creamy bases. It's great mixed into yogurt, as a coating for a soft farm cheese, or whisked into a buttermilk salad dressing. The mushroom version here is not technically a za'atar on its own, but when we pair it with some fresh savory leaves, it has the same effect and adds a boost of umami to whatever you're seasoning.

Note: You can use store-bought dried herbs for these recipes, but we dry our own herbs at Bavel for added freshness and flavor. To do the same at home, place sprigs of fresh marjoram and thyme in a food dehydrator at 110°F for 24 hours, then pulverize the leaves in a spice grinder or food processor. Citric acid is an organic acid found naturally in citrus fruit. It can be purchased in powdered form to add a sour flavor to foods and drinks.

Rose Za'atar

MAKES ABOUT ⅓ CUP

2 teaspoons untoasted
  black sesame seeds

1 tablespoon coarsely
  ground dried rose petals

1 tablespoon finely
  ground dried marjoram

1 tablespoon finely
  ground dried thyme

1 tablespoon plus 1½ teaspoons
  ground sumac

2 teaspoons black sesame seeds,
  toasted (see page 20)

½ teaspoon citric acid

½ teaspoon granulated sugar

¾ teaspoon kosher salt

3 drops food-grade rose oil

In a mortar and pestle or a spice grinder, crush the untoasted sesame seeds until they form a coarse meal. Grind the rose petals in a spice grinder or food processor until roughly chopped.

In a bowl, combine the ground sesame seeds, ground rose petals, marjoram, thyme, sumac, toasted sesame seeds, citric acid, sugar, salt, and rose oil and mix by hand, rubbing the mixture between your fingers to break up any clumps and rehydrate the herbs with the sesame and rose oils. This will keep the za'atar fresh for longer. Store in an airtight container at room temperature for 2 to 3 weeks.

Mushroom Za'atar

MAKES ABOUT ⅓ CUP

2 tablespoons plus 1 teaspoon black
  sesame seeds, toasted (see page 20)

2 tablespoons oyster mushroom
  powder (may substitute any mixture
  of store-bought dried mushrooms,
  ground to a powder)

1 teaspoon kosher salt

2 tablespoons ground sumac

In a bowl, combine the sesame seeds, mushroom powder, salt, and sumac and mix together. Store in an airtight container at room temperature for 2 to 3 weeks.

Hawaij

Hawaij is a delicious currylike spice blend from Yemen that you'll find seasoning all kinds of traditional Yemeni stews, rice dishes, vegetables, and even coffee. I had a lot of Yemeni friends growing up, and I remember spending the night at their houses on Friday and waking up on Saturday morning to the smell of hawaij-spiced feasts of lusty Yemeni dishes. You can use hawaij the same way you'd use any curry powder, in the base of a stew or a curry, rubbed onto meats, or mixed into a sauce for cooking vegetables, as we do with our cauliflower at Bavel.

MAKES ABOUT ¼ CUP

1 tablespoon ground turmeric
1 tablespoon plus 1 teaspoon
  ground cumin
2 teaspoons ground cardamom
1 tablespoon plus 1 teaspoon
  ground coriander
1½ teaspoons freshly ground
  black pepper

Add the turmeric, cumin, cardamom, coriander, and pepper to a small bowl and stir to combine. Store in an airtight container at room temperature for 2 to 3 weeks.

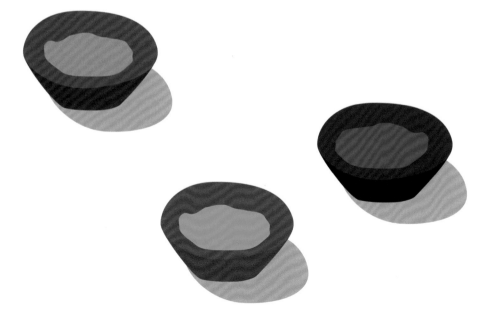

Ras el Hanout

There's no singular recipe for ras el hanout. The name translates literally to "head of the shop"—sort of like "top shelf"—and is a catchall term for a Moroccan spice shop's signature all-purpose blend. Vendors pride themselves on the sheer number of different ingredients mixed into their ras el hanout; most recipes tout at least twelve ingredients, and I've seen some go as high as twenty-five. But—and I may piss off half of my relatives when I say this—I honestly think that's too many. With so many spices mixed together, the flavor can become murky and one-note. So, the ras el hanout at Bavel has just seven spices—which is still more than any other seasoning we use but restrained enough to maintain balance and nuance. Our ras el hanout goes into the base of our Beef Cheek Tagine (page 213) and is excellent with any similarly slow-cooked stew. It's also excellent rubbed onto meats and fish or sprinkled into couscous or rice while it cooks.

MAKES ABOUT ¼ CUP

1 tablespoon plus 1 teaspoon
  ground paprika
½ teaspoon ground cloves
1½ teaspoons ground cardamom
1 tablespoon ground cumin
1 tablespoon ground turmeric
1 tablespoon plus 1 teaspoon
  ground coriander
2 teaspoons ground Kashmiri pepper
  (may substitute cayenne)

Add the paprika, cloves, cardamom, cumin, turmeric, coriander, and Kashmiri pepper to a small bowl and stir to combine. Store in an airtight container at room temperature for 2 to 3 weeks.

Shawarma Spice Blend

My favorite shawarma in all of Tel Aviv comes from a little place called Dr. Shakshuka, run by a guy named Bino Gabso—aka the doctor. As his restaurant's name suggests, Bino started out making only shakshuka—the classic breakfast dish of eggs cooked in a rich tomato sauce. Eventually, though, he opened a little shawarma spot in back, and that's where you'll find what I consider the best shawarma in the city and the inspiration for the flavors in Bavel's shawarma spice blend.

Dr. Shakshuka uses cuts of lamb and beef that are stacked and roasted on a spit and then shaved into warm pita. At Bavel, what we call our lamb neck shawarma (page 207) is oven-roasted rather than spit-roasted, but it still has all of those same meaty, crispy, fatty, chewy qualities. The spice blend's warm mix of allspice, nutmeg, and cinnamon pairs really well with the lamb, with a big hit of sumac to cut through the richness. You can use this mix to brighten up any rich, fatty cut of meat, from lamb to braised oxtails.

MAKES ABOUT ¼ CUP

2 teaspoons ground sumac
1 tablespoon ground cardamom
1½ teaspoons ground allspice
½ teaspoon nutmeg, grated with a Microplane
2½ teaspoons ground cinnamon

Add the sumac, cardamom, allspice, nutmeg, and cinnamon to a small bowl and stir to combine. Store in an airtight container at room temperature for 2 to 3 weeks.

Poultry Spice Blend

The Middle East and Asia share a common spice heritage—the result of millennia of trading along the ancient Silk Road. The star anise in this blend is part of that connection, and when mixed with the cinnamon and orange peel, it has hints of a Chinese five-spice blend. We also add cardamom and sumac, the acid of which helps to offset the richness of fattier meats, like the aged duck (page 199) we serve this with at Bavel.

MAKES ABOUT ¼ CUP

1¼ teaspoons ground dried orange peel
1 teaspoon ground cardamom
1 tablespoon plus 1 teaspoon ground sumac
1 teaspoon ground star anise
2 teaspoons ground cinnamon

Add the orange peel, cardamom, sumac, star anise, and cinnamon to a small bowl and stir to combine. Use immediately or store in an airtight container at room temperature for 2 to 3 weeks.

Jerusalem Spice Blends

Growing up, my dad used to take me to this hole-in-the-wall restaurant in Jerusalem's Mahane Yehuda Market called Hatzot, which was supposedly the birthplace of the Jerusalem mixed-grill sandwich. You'll find versions of it at shops throughout the country, but they're all a riff on the original, in which bits of chicken offal—liver, heart, spleen, gizzard—and thighs are seared on a griddle, topped with a pile of caramelized onions, seasoned with a special spice mix, and shoved into a pita that's smeared with a little bit of hummus. As a kid, I remember it always came with two pickles on the side, and on the table, there would be a little squeeze bottle with amba, the tart pickled mango chutney, to finish it off. It's as good as it sounds—rich, salty, spicy, sweet—and every time, I'd eat two whole sandwiches and just be ruined for the rest of the day. It was worth it.

My hands, too, would bear the orange scars of the spice mix that's become the sandwich's signature element. Heavy with turmeric, paprika, and cumin, it stains the chicken bits and juices an orangey-red while tempering the minerally funk of the offal, and today, every place with a Jerusalem mixed-grill sandwich makes its own blend. At Bavel, we have two versions: the traditional red and a milder brighter green blend—with hints of orange, ginger, and fennel—that goes well with duck, as a marinade for grilled or roasted chicken, or as a seasoning for roasted potatoes.

Red Jerusalem Spice Blend

MAKES ABOUT ¼ CUP

1 tablespoon plus 1 teaspoon ground mustard seeds
2 teaspoons ground cumin
1 teaspoon ground chile flakes
½ teaspoon ground fenugreek
1 teaspoon paprika
½ teaspoon ground turmeric

Add the mustard seeds, cumin, chile flakes, fenugreek, paprika, and turmeric to a small bowl and stir to combine. Use immediately or store in an airtight container at room temperature for 2 to 3 weeks.

Green Jerusalem Spice Blend

MAKES ABOUT ¼ CUP

1 teaspoon ground dried orange peel
2 teaspoons ground cumin
1 teaspoon ground coriander
½ teaspoon ground fennel seeds
1 teaspoon ground dried mint
½ teaspoon ground ginger
½ teaspoon freshly ground black pepper

Add the orange peel, cumin, coriander, fennel seeds, mint, ginger, and pepper to a small bowl and stir to combine. Use immediately or store in an airtight container at room temperature for 2 to 3 weeks.

Pepita & White Sesame Dukkah

Dukkah is all about texture. When crunched between your teeth, the mixture of seeds, nuts, and whole spices pops with fat and flavor, adding depth and dimension to dishes that might otherwise be one-note. It's like a Middle Eastern gremolata. Dukkah originated in Egypt, and throughout the Middle East, you'll find variations scattered over warm bread or mixed with olive oil for dipping.

MAKES ABOUT 2 CUPS

¼ cup grapeseed oil
1 cup pepitas (pumpkin seeds)
¼ cup whole coriander seeds
½ cup white sesame seeds
¾ teaspoon kosher salt

Line a sheet pan with paper towels. In a 10-inch sauté pan, add the oil, pepitas, and coriander seeds. Place the pan on the stove over high heat and fry the seeds for 2 minutes, until they pop and the pepitas start to swell and develop a golden color. Then add the sesame seeds to the pan and fry for 2 minutes more, until the sesame seeds turn a light golden brown. Remove from the heat, add the salt, and stir to combine. Pour the mixture onto the prepared sheet pan to drain the excess oil and to let cool. Use immediately or store in an airtight container for up to 5 days.

Baharat Spice Blend

The name "baharat" comes from the Arabic word for "spice." This blend originated in North Africa and is widely used in Saudi Arabia and Turkey. Baharat spices can be used for sweet or savory cooking. This blend has been specifically made for use in pastry, omitting any spices that would be jarring in a dessert.

MAKES 2 TEASPOONS (DOUBLE THIS
IF USING FOR DUSTING)

¾ teaspoon ground cardamom
½ teaspoon ground cinnamon
¼ teaspoon finely ground
  black pepper
¼ teaspoon ground star anise
Lightly rounded ⅛ teaspoon
  ground nutmeg

In a small bowl, add the cardamom, cinnamon, pepper, star anise, and nutmeg and stir to combine. The spice blend can be added to the financier batter (see headnote, page 259), or as we do in the restaurant, dusted on top of the completed dessert. Store in an airtight container for up to 2 weeks.

Garam Masala

There is no one recipe for garam masala; like most all of the world's great spice blends, there are a zillion different versions, each skewed depending on geography (every region of the Indian subcontinent has its own), tradition, and personal taste. The unifying quality, though, is warmth—a fragrant spice blend's almost wintery aroma that comes from the key players like cinnamon, nutmeg, cloves, and cardamom.

One of Bavel's sous chefs, Johnny Cirelle, came up with this particular garam masala mix, which stars as the unexpected surprise in Bavel's tabbouleh. I add it to the Golden Balsamic Mushroom Vinaigrette (page 107), where it lends a perfume to the normally mild mix of bulgur and herbs, and to the Green Herb Sauce (page 203) that tops our lamb chops. Although it's commonly used in slow-cooked stews and sauces, I find the flavors of garam masala get muddied when they cook for too long, so I generally like to use it at the end, as an intense, flavorful finisher.

MAKES ½ CUP

2 tablespoons freshly
  ground black pepper
2 tablespoons ground cardamom
1 tablespoon plus 1 teaspoon
  ground cinnamon
1 teaspoon ground cumin
½ teaspoon ground coriander
½ teaspoon nutmeg, grated with
  a Microplane
2 tablespoons ground cloves

Add the pepper, cardamom, cinnamon, cumin, coriander, nutmeg, and cloves to a small bowl and stir to combine. Use immediately or store in an airtight container at room temperature for 2 to 3 weeks.

Sauces

The chutney and zhougs in this chapter are a nod to the lineup of condiments you would find at most Middle Eastern street stands to help add flavor and complexity to whatever you're eating. At Bavel, we use them the same way, to add a final note of acid, heat, and vibrancy to a finished dish.

Mint Chutney

There is a casual Peruvian restaurant chain here in L.A. called Pollo A la Brasa. They serve this incredible smoky grilled chicken that comes with a spicy aji verde, a green sauce made of serranos, habaneros, and garlic. It's so good—enhancing the flavor of the chicken without overwhelming it and leaving you wanting more. When we first started cooking the lamb neck shawarma (page 207) at Bavel, it came with pickles and tahini, but it needed something spicy. I went to Pollo A la Brasa for lunch one day and realized that their sauce was exactly what I was looking for. This chutney is inspired by that Peruvian aji verde, with habaneros, garlic, and other spices, with the addition of fresh mint and crème fraîche to pair with the lamb.

MAKES ¾ CUP

1 tablespoon plus 1 teaspoon Green Jerusalem Spice Blend (page 32)

½ cup packed cilantro leaves, chopped

¾ cup packed mint leaves, chopped

½ Persian cucumber, roughly chopped

3 tablespoons crème fraîche

1-inch piece fresh ginger, peeled

1 teaspoon kosher salt

3 garlic cloves

2 tablespoons plus 1 teaspoon freshly squeezed lemon juice

¼ cup olive oil

1 large habanero pepper, roughly chopped (seeds removed, if desired)

1 tablespoon amba (pickled mango paste*)

Combine the spice blend, cilantro, mint, cucumber, crème fraîche, ginger, salt, garlic, lemon juice, oil, pepper, and mango paste in a blender and puree on high for 45 to 60 seconds, until just smooth. (Stop as soon as it's fully pureed or the mixture will brown.) Store in an airtight container in the refrigerator for up to 2 days.

Our preferred brand of pickled mango paste is Galil.

Zhougs

Zhoug is to shawarma what salsa is to tacos—hot, addictive, and a sharp contrast to whatever rich, fatty thing it comes in contact with. Originally from Yemen, the fiery condiment has a dense, round flavor that comes from a variety of fresh chiles, herbs, and spices. I make three different zhougs at Bavel: my green version is a thicker take on a classic version normally made with a mix of fresh and dried chiles and heavy with cumin and cardamom. Normally, green zhoug is highly acidic, oxidizing quickly, so it needs to be made fresh daily. This version is more of a paste than a sauce, and the low acid and high spice prevent it from oxidizing, so you can keep it for weeks. The longer it sits, the more aroma and flavor it develops. The red zhoug is just as intense and also sweet from the fried peppers that make up its base. I like to spoon a bit of these first two over my hummus, then swipe a bit of pita through them one at a time. My third zhoug, a strawberry version, is the least traditional and also the hottest of the three, with red chile flakes and the subtle, floral sweetness of ripe berries. This one I swirl into crème fraîche along with grated tomato and dill to accompany a warm sheet of flaky Malawach (page 166).

Red Zhoug

MAKES 1 CUP

1 cup grapeseed oil

2 large red bell peppers, stemmed and seeded, cut into 8 pieces

8 Fresno chiles,* stemmed and seeded, cut in half

1 tablespoon plus 1 teaspoon ground paprika

1 teaspoon ground turmeric

¼ teaspoon ground cloves

1 teaspoon ground green cardamom pods, with the husks (see page 20)

½ teaspoon ground cumin

2 teaspoons kosher salt

3 garlic cloves, grated with a Microplane

1 tablespoon plus 1 teaspoon freshly squeezed lemon juice

2 tablespoons packed cilantro leaves, chopped

Add the oil to a large sauté pan and place on the stove over high heat. Once the oil is hot, add the bell peppers and chiles and fry while continuously stirring for about 10 minutes, until the peppers start to blister and darken in color. If at any time the peppers start to burn, decrease the heat slightly.

Remove the peppers and chiles from the oil, set aside, and let cool. Add the cooled fried peppers and chiles and the paprika, turmeric, cloves, cardamom, cumin, salt, garlic, and lemon juice to a food processor and blend, stopping to scrape down the sides of the bowl with a spatula when necessary, until the mixture is the consistency of a chunky puree, about 2 minutes. Transfer to a bowl and set aside to cool, then add the cilantro and stir to combine. Store in an airtight container in the refrigerator for up to 2 weeks.

The spice level of Fresno chiles can vary. If you'd like more heat, stir in ½ to 1 teaspoon cayenne or ground chile flakes.

Green Zhoug

MAKES ½ CUP

1½ teaspoons kosher salt

2 garlic cloves

2 serrano chiles with seeds,
  roughly chopped

1 cup packed parsley leaves, chopped

1½ cups packed cilantro leaves,
  chopped

3 tablespoons plus 1 teaspoon
  Hawaij (page 26)

1 tablespoon jalapeño powder*

1 tablespoon freshly squeezed
  lemon juice

1½ teaspoons sherry vinegar

3 tablespoons olive oil

In a mortar and pestle, combine the salt, garlic, and chiles and mash to a paste. Add the parsley and cilantro and continue to mash. Then add the hawaij, jalapeño powder, lemon juice, and vinegar and gently stir to combine. Finally, add the oil and gently stir to incorporate. Store in an airtight container in the refrigerator for up to 3 weeks.

Strawberry Zhoug

MAKES ¾ CUP

1½ cups (12 ounces) strawberries,
  stemmed

1 tablespoon plus 2 teaspoons
  strawberry liqueur (optional)

2 tablespoons plus 2 teaspoons
  Hawaij (page 26)

1 tablespoon ground chile flakes

1 garlic clove, grated with
  a Microplane

1 teaspoon kosher salt

Pinch of citric acid

Add the strawberries to a blender and puree on high until smooth.

In a small saucepan over medium-low heat, add the strawberry puree, strawberry liqueur (if using), hawaij, chile flakes, and garlic. Cook, stirring continuously to keep from scorching, for about 10 minutes, until thickened, dark red, and reduced by half.

Pour the reduced puree into a small bowl, add the salt and citric acid, and stir to combine. Let cool to room temperature, then store in an airtight container in the refrigerator for up to a month.

We use jalapeño powder to keep the water content low; this results in a thicker paste. You can substitute 1 fresh jalapeño for the powder or, to make your own powder, place 6 jalapeños in a dehydrator at 110°F for 24 hours, then pulse in a spice grinder or coffee grinder or grind in a mortar and pestle. Store in an airtight container for up to 3 months. If you choose to use a fresh jalapeño, the consistency of the zhoug will be a little looser.

Stocks

In the Middle East, the base of many recipes starts with protein, vegetables, and spices covered in water. This is good, but there are techniques for extracting even more flavor, like using stock in place of water for double the impact.

Vegetable Stock

Vegetable stock is so simple to make, but it's one of those small things that makes a big impact when used in place of water for everything from thinning out sauces to cooking stews and grains.

MAKES ABOUT 2 QUARTS

¼ cup grapeseed oil
2 large yellow onions, chopped
2 large carrots, peeled and chopped
2 celery ribs, trimmed and chopped
5 fresh bay leaves or 2 dry bay leaves
15 black peppercorns
3 stems flat-leaf parsley
3 quarts water
1 whole garlic head, halved crosswise
2 sprigs thyme

Preheat a large stockpot over low heat, then pour in the oil and increase the heat to high. Add the onions, carrots, and celery and let them sear, stirring occasionally, for about 2 minutes. Add the bay leaves and peppercorns and cook until the vegetables are lightly caramelized and golden brown but not burned, about 10 minutes. Add the parsley and water. Cover the pot and bring to a boil. Once boiling, remove the lid and add the garlic. Turn the heat to low and simmer gently, uncovered, until the liquid has reduced by one-third, about 1½ hours.

Remove the pot from the heat. Add the thyme and let sit for 10 minutes. Using an extra-fine-mesh strainer or chinois, strain the stock into an airtight container. Discard the solids. Use immediately or let the stock cool to room temperature, cover tightly, and refrigerate for up to 5 days or freeze for up to 3 months.

Super Stock

We call this our super stock because of its extra aromatics, which include ginger, lime leaf, cilantro, chiles, and fish sauce. At Bavel, we use this for our beef cheek, but at home, I love to cook rice in it or add it to the base of a simple curry.

MAKES ABOUT 2 QUARTS

2 quarts Vegetable Stock (see left)

3½-inch piece fresh ginger, peeled and julienned

8 makrut lime leaves, julienned

15 cilantro stems

2 fresh bay leaves, julienned, or 1 dry bay leaf, crumbled

5 garlic cloves, smashed

1 Fresno chile, halved lengthwise

1 tablespoon plus 2 teaspoons fish sauce

In a large stockpot, bring the vegetable stock to a boil. Add the ginger, lime leaves, cilantro, bay leaves, garlic, chile, and fish sauce, then remove from the heat and let steep, uncovered, for 30 minutes.

Using an extra-fine-mesh strainer or chinois, strain the stock into an airtight container or containers. Discard the solids. Use immediately or let the stock cool to room temperature, cover tightly, and refrigerate for up to 5 days or freeze for up to 3 months.

Duck Broth

The aged duck (page 199) we serve at Bavel calls for the legs and breast of two ducks, and I like to use the carcasses to make duck broth. I throw in some dried mushrooms, green onion, garlic, and some burnt tomato for color, then simmer it low for 4 hours. The result is a heady, comforting broth that you can sip all by itself.

MAKES ABOUT 4 QUARTS

SPECIAL
EQUIPMENT:

Cheesecloth

5¼ pounds duck bones (or the carcasses of 2 whole ducks, reserved from Aged Duck, page 199)

5 quarts plus 1½ cups water

½ small tomato

3 green onions, white and light green parts only, roughly chopped, green tops reserved

2 garlic cloves, thinly sliced

¼ yellow onion, roughly chopped

1-inch piece fresh ginger, peeled and sliced

¼ cup (¼ ounce) mixed dried mushrooms

Kosher salt, to taste

Using kitchen shears or a cleaver, cut each carcass into six even pieces. Add the bones and water to a large stockpot. Bring to a simmer over high heat, then decrease the heat to low and simmer for 15 minutes, periodically using a slotted spoon to skim off any impurities that rise to the surface. Meanwhile, in a cast-iron or other heavy skillet over high heat, char the tomato cut-side down.

Add the green onion, garlic, yellow onion, and the charred tomato to the stockpot and continue to simmer, periodically skimming off any impurities that rise to the surface, for 4 hours and 15 minutes, or until the broth is golden in color and slightly viscous.

Remove the pot from the heat and add the ginger, mushrooms, and the reserved green onion tops. Let sit for another 15 minutes, off the heat, to infuse.

Strain the broth through a cheesecloth-lined colander or chinois into a bowl. Season with salt and serve, or transfer to an airtight container, and refrigerate for up to 5 days or freeze for up to 3 months.

Turmeric-Chicken Stock

My grandmother always added turmeric to the base of her chicken soup. It was, like most of the food she grew up with, peasant food, but that little bit of golden color added a vibrancy that made it feel special. Turmeric has a ruddy, almost rustlike minerality that's deeply savory and nicely balances the sweet onions, carrots, and celery in the stock.

MAKES ABOUT 4 QUARTS

SPECIAL
EQUIPMENT:

Cheesecloth

5 pounds mixed chicken bones
6 quarts water
½ small tomato
2 yellow onions, large diced
2 carrots, peeled and large diced
3 celery ribs, trimmed and large diced
2 fresh bay leaves, torn,
   or 1 dry bay leaf
1 teaspoon black peppercorns
6-inch piece fresh turmeric,
   peeled and sliced
5 sprigs flat-leaf parsley
1 small tomato, halved
1 whole garlic head, halved crosswise
½ teaspoon ground turmeric

Add the chicken bones and water to a large stockpot. Place over high heat and bring to a slow boil, then decrease the heat to low and simmer for 15 minutes, periodically skimming off any impurities that rise to the surface with a slotted spoon.

Meanwhile, in a cast-iron or other heavy skillet over high heat, char the tomato cut-side down.

Add the onions, carrots, celery, bay leaves, and peppercorns to the stockpot and continue to simmer, periodically skimming off the impurities, for another 3¼ hours. Add the sliced turmeric, parsley, the charred tomato, garlic, and ground turmeric and simmer for 30 more minutes.

Remove the pot from the heat and discard the bones. Line a colander or chinois with cheesecloth that has been folded into three or four layers. Strain the stock through the prepared colander into a large container.

Use immediately or let the stock cool to room temperature, cover tightly, and refrigerate for up to 5 days or freeze for up to 3 months.

Pickles & Ferments

In the Middle East, a region renowned for its heat, techniques like pickling and preserving were essential to keeping produce fresh before refrigeration, and they have evolved to become a key part of the cuisine. These tangy ingredients help cut through rich meats and bring balance to a dish. I use a variety of pickles in everything, from a simple chopped salad to the lamb neck shawarma (page 207) at Bavel, but mostly I like to have a pickle plate in the middle of the table to snack on throughout a meal, for whenever your palate needs a quick hit of brightness and crunch.

Marinated Olives

At Bavel, we use a mix of four different types of olives: picholine, gaeta, castelvetrano, and mantequilla, but any variety of brine-cured olives would work for this recipe.

MAKES 4 CUPS

SPECIAL
EQUIPMENT:

*Candy or other
probe-style
thermometer*

2 star anise

2 cinnamon sticks

1 teaspoon whole fennel seeds

1½ cups olive oil

2 dried morita chiles (may substitute
   dried chipotle peppers)

1 garlic clove, thinly sliced

1 fresh bay leaf, torn, or
   1 dry bay leaf, torn

2 sprigs thyme

1 sprig savory (may substitute
   oregano or marjoram)

Zest of ½ Meyer or regular lemon
   and the lemon thinly sliced

Zest of ½ lime and the lime
   thinly sliced

Zest of ½ orange and the orange
   thinly sliced

4 cups mixed olives, drained

Feta cheese for serving

Preheat the oven to 375°F. Evenly spread the star anise, cinnamon sticks, and fennel seeds on a dry sheet pan and toast for 4 minutes, until the aroma of the spices is very fragrant.

In a small saucepan fitted with a candy thermometer, combine the oil, chiles, garlic, bay leaf, thyme, and savory. Then add the toasted spices and the lemon, lime, and orange zest slices. Cook on medium-low heat to gently infuse. Once the thermometer reaches 230°F, remove the pan from the heat and let it sit until the temperature drops to 110°F, about 30 minutes, then add the olives. Allow the olives to marinate at room temperature for 2 hours, then refrigerate overnight. Store the olives in the marinade in an airtight container in the refrigerator for up to 3 months.

When ready to serve, remove the olives from the refrigerator and bring to room temperature. Drain the olives from the oil (you can add this oil back to the olive marinade or use it to cook with). Place the drained olives in a bowl and top with a few olive-size pieces of crumbled feta.

Pickled Cucumbers

This pickle is an updated version of the ones my dad used to make for me as a kid when I was growing up.

MAKES 1 GALLON

SPECIAL
EQUIPMENT:

*One-gallon
jar with lid*

4 pounds Persian cucumbers

2 Fresno chiles, halved lengthwise,
    seeds included

1½-inch piece fresh turmeric,
    peeled and thinly sliced

10 sprigs dill

4 innermost celery ribs, with leaves

2 teaspoons black peppercorns

3-inch piece fresh ginger, unpeeled
    and thinly sliced

1 whole garlic head, halved crosswise

3 fresh bay leaves or 2 dry bay leaves

1 cup room temperature water

½ cup plus 1 teaspoon kosher salt

½ cup plus 3 tablespoons
    granulated sugar

5 cups plus 2 tablespoons water

1½ cups white wine vinegar

1½ cups champagne vinegar

Add the cucumbers, chiles, turmeric, dill, celery, peppercorns, ginger, garlic, and bay leaves to a 1-gallon jar and pack down tightly with a spoon or your hands.

In a large bowl, combine the room temperature water, salt, and sugar and stir until the salt and sugar have dissolved. Then add the additional water and white wine and champagne vinegars to the bowl and stir to combine.

Pour the pickling liquid into the jar and seal. Let the jar sit at room temperature for 5 to 7 days before use. Store the jar in the refrigerator for up to 3 months.

Turmeric Pickled Cauliflower

Cauliflower is a perfect canvas for the yellow tint of turmeric. It is a vegetable that doesn't have much flavor, but absorbs liquid really well to create a vibrantly flavored pickle.

MAKES ½ GALLON

SPECIAL
EQUIPMENT:

*Half-gallon
jar with lid*

One 1½-pound cauliflower,
   cut into 1-inch florets
1 teaspoon brown mustard seeds
2 teaspoons ground turmeric
1-inch piece fresh turmeric,
   unpeeled and thinly sliced
1 tablespoon Red Jerusalem
   Spice Mix (page 32)
½ teaspoon ground dried orange peel
2 tablespoons amba (pickled
   mango paste)
1 Fresno chile, halved lengthwise,
   seeds included
1½ cups plus 3 tablespoons
   champagne vinegar
1½ cups plus 3 tablespoons
   white wine vinegar
3½ cups plus 3 tablespoons water
½ cup granulated sugar
2 tablespoons plus 2 teaspoons
   kosher salt

In a half-gallon jar, combine the cauliflower, mustard seeds, ground turmeric, fresh turmeric, spice mix, orange peel, mango paste, and chile and pack down tightly with a spoon or your hands.

In a saucepan, combine the champagne and white wine vinegars, water, sugar, and salt and bring to a boil.

Pour the pickling liquid into the jar and fill to the top. Let the jar sit, uncovered, until it reaches room temperature, about 45 minutes. Seal the jar and let it sit at room temperature for 2 days before use. Store the jar in the refrigerator for up to 3 months.

Beet-Pickled Turnips

These are very similar to the beet-colored pickled turnips you would find in a falafel shop with multiple layers of flavor from the herbs, chiles, and vinegars that we add to the brine.

MAKES ½ GALLON

SPECIAL
EQUIPMENT:

*Half-gallon
jar with lid*

7 cups (about 17 small) Tokyo turnips, quartered on a bias (may substitute any small baby turnips)

1 Fresno chile, halved lengthwise, seeds included

2 fresh bay leaves or 1 dry bay leaf

3 sprigs dill, chopped

1 whole garlic head, halved crosswise

½ teaspoon black peppercorns

1 large red beet, peeled and sliced

1½ cups plus 3 tablespoons champagne vinegar

1½ cups plus 3 tablespoons white wine vinegar

3½ cups plus 3 tablespoons water

6 tablespoons plus 2 teaspoons granulated sugar

3 tablespoons plus 2 teaspoons kosher salt

In a half-gallon jar, combine the turnips, chile, bay leaves, dill, garlic, peppercorns, and beet and pack down tightly with a spoon or your hands.

In a saucepan, combine the champagne and white wine vinegars, water, sugar, and salt and bring to a boil.

Pour the pickling liquid into the jar and fill to the top. Let the jar sit, uncovered, until it reaches room temperature, about 45 minutes. Seal the jar and let sit at room temperature for 5 to 7 days before use. Store in the refrigerator for up to 3 months.

Pickled Okra

My grandma's favorite vegetable is okra, and I love cooking with it, too. By pickling the pods, you reduce some of their inherent sliminess, and the mix of Indian spices showcases how versatile okra can be.

Note: To choose okra that is not fibrous, pick one up and snap it. If it bends but doesn't snap, it's too fibrous.

MAKES ½ GALLON

SPECIAL
EQUIPMENT:

*Half-gallon
jar with lid*

1 small yellow onion, sliced into rings

1 pound okra

2 small Fresno chiles, halved lengthwise, seeds included

2 small serrano chiles, halved lengthwise, seeds included

1-inch piece fresh turmeric, unpeeled and thinly sliced

2-inch piece fresh ginger, unpeeled and thinly sliced

20 small curry leaves

1½ teaspoons brown mustard seeds, toasted

1 tablespoon plus 2 teaspoons Hawaij (page 26)

3 tablespoons kosher salt

5 tablespoons granulated sugar

3 cups plus 1 tablespoon water

¾ cup champagne vinegar

¾ cup white wine vinegar

In a half-gallon jar, starting with the onion, alternate layers of the onion and okra in the jar, making sure to finish with the onion on top to weigh down the okra in the liquid.

Add the Fresno and serrano chiles, turmeric, ginger, curry leaves, and mustard seeds to the jar.

In a saucepan, combine the hawaij, salt, sugar, water, and the champagne and white wine vinegars and bring to a boil.

Pour the pickling liquid into the jar and fill to the top. Seal the jar and let sit at room temperature for 5 days before use. Store in the refrigerator for up to 3 months.

Pickled Celery

Israeli salad typically uses pickled cucumber, but I started making one with celery instead, and it's incredible. Try topping a hamburger with pickled celery—it's amazing.

MAKES ½ GALLON

SPECIAL EQUIPMENT:

Half-gallon jar with lid

1½ pounds celery, top leaves trimmed and ribs sliced on a bias into ½-inch-thick slices

20 small curry leaves

½ teaspoon black peppercorns

2 teaspoons coriander seeds, toasted

1 teaspoon yellow mustard seeds

4 green cardamom pods, toasted

1 Fresno chile, halved lengthwise, seeds included

4 garlic cloves, halved

2 teaspoons ground turmeric

1 tablespoon fish sauce

1½ cups plus 3 tablespoons champagne vinegar

1½ cups plus 3 tablespoons white wine vinegar

3½ cups plus 3 tablespoons water

6 tablespoons plus 2 teaspoons granulated sugar

3 tablespoons plus 2 teaspoons kosher salt

In a half-gallon jar, combine the celery, curry leaves, peppercorns, coriander seeds, mustard seeds, cardamom, chile, garlic, turmeric, and fish sauce and pack down tightly with a spoon or your hands.

In a saucepan, combine the champagne and white wine vinegars, water, sugar, and salt and bring to a boil.

Pour the pickling liquid into the jar and fill to the top. Let the jar sit, uncovered, until it reaches room temperature, about 45 minutes. Seal the jar and let sit at room temperature for 2 days before use. Store in the refrigerator for up to 3 months.

Fermented Cabbage

L.A. has one of the most vibrant Koreatowns in the world, and you can taste its influence in this cabbage, which is fermented using a technique similar to kimchi, but with flavors of the Middle East—a perfect hybrid of where I come from and where I live now.

MAKES ½ GALLON

SPECIAL EQUIPMENT:

One-gallon jar with lid

3 pounds cabbage, cored and quartered

3 tablespoons kosher salt, divided

2 teaspoons fish sauce (may substitute ½ teaspoon kosher salt)

4 garlic cloves, grated with a Microplane

3 tablespoons Red Jerusalem Spice Blend (page 32)

Shred the cabbage by cutting it from the short end (bottom) into ¼-inch-thick slices. Wash the cabbage in cold water, then dry thoroughly in a salad spinner or on paper towels.

In a 1-gallon jar, add half the cabbage and 1 tablespoon plus 2 teaspoons (15g) of the salt and shake to coat. Then add the remaining cabbage to the jar, followed by the remaining 1 tablespoon plus 1 teaspoon (12g) salt. Add the fish sauce, then seal the jar and shake to thoroughly coat the cabbage. Move to a cold, dark place and turn the jar upside down and then back right side up five times each day for 7 days.

After 7 days, open the jar. The cabbage may have a slightly funky smell to it, depending on the minerality of the cabbage. Then add the garlic and spice blend. Using a glove to protect your hand, massage the cabbage with the spice mixture to completely coat. Transfer the cabbage to a ½-gallon jar, seal the jar and let refrigerate for 24 hours before use. Store in the refrigerator for up to 3 months.

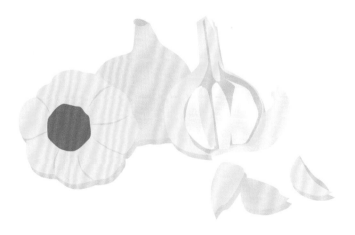

Preserved Meyer Lemons

A constant presence in my pantry growing up, preserved lemon is another one of those staples that I rely on to add brightness and depth. Its savory tartness is sour and bitter but also floral and sweet, hitting your palate in many places at once. A little bit can take a dish from being average to magnificent.

MAKES 1 GALLON

SPECIAL
EQUIPMENT:

*One-gallon
jar with lid*

5½ pounds (about 18 ripe, not soft) Meyer lemons, cleaned (may substitute regular lemons)

5⅓ cups kosher salt

4 cups freshly squeezed Meyer lemon juice (may substitute regular lemon juice)

If all of the lemons don't fit, add as many as you can. After 1 day, the lemons will have shrunk some, and then you should be able to fit in the remaining lemons.

Cut the stems off the tops of the lemons. Then cut the lemons into quarters, through the lemon but not all the way through, leaving about ½ inch intact at the base.

Place the salt on a small sheet pan. Holding the lemons over the pan, stuff them with the salt so the pan catches any excess salt.

Pack the salted lemons into a 1-gallon jar, pressing them in so they fit as tightly as possible.* The pressure of their being tightly packed will force the lemons to release liquid. Then take the remaining salt left on the pan and pour it over the lemons in the jar.

Seal the jar and mark it with a date. Let the jar sit for 24 hours at room temperature to release liquid. Then uncover the jar and add the lemon juice. If 4 cups is not enough to cover the lemons, add more lemon juice. Seal the jar again and let it sit for 1½ months at room temperature (2 to 2½ months if using regular lemons), then store in the refrigerator for up to 6 months.

To use: Remove a lemon from the jar and rinse under cold water for 20 seconds. Cut out the lemon flesh and discard or use it in a vinaigrette. Use the peels (with the pith) sliced thinly, as your recipe suggests.

Dips & Spreads

Before the platter of kebabs or roasted lamb arrives on the Middle Eastern dinner table, there's usually a whole delicious preamble that happens first: tangy, umami-dense dips like baba ghanoush, labneh, and hummus join other vegetable mezze and fresh flatbread to form a tempting distraction from the main course ahead. I remember as a kid, I'd often be so full from scarfing these luscious, creamy starters that I wouldn't have room for the main course at all. And when swiped through with a warm flatbread, these flavorful spreads can be a satisfying meal all on their own.

Tahini

In Middle Eastern cooking, the word "tahini" refers to both the paste made from ground white sesame seeds and the creamy condiment that's made with it. This recipe is for the latter and calls for tahini paste that gets mixed with garlic, lemon, salt, and ice water to form a rich, silky dip that's ideal with warm pita, grilled meat, or anything in a sandwich. My tahini is a lot thicker than what you normally find when it's used to add a cool creaminess to shawarma or sabich. This version might be too heavy on that kind of sandwich (though you can thin it out with some lemon juice and water), but its smooth texture and delicate flavor is worth eating on its own, the way my dad always served it.

Note: The ice in this recipe serves a dual purpose. It keeps the ingredients cold as they mix, which prevents the sesame from turning bitter and also helps to aerate the tahini to achieve a whipped, almost mayonnaise-like texture.

MAKES 4 CUPS

2 large garlic cloves, grated
  with a Microplane
2 tablespoons freshly
  squeezed lemon juice
2¼ cups raw tahini paste
2 cups ice water
1 tablespoon kosher salt
Black sesame seeds, toasted
  (see page 20), for garnish
Olive oil for garnish
Whole-Wheat Pita (page 157)
  for serving

In a small bowl, combine the garlic and lemon juice and let sit for 3 minutes. Then add the mixture to a food processor along with the tahini and 1 cup of the ice water (including the ice), and puree. Once the mixture thickens to a pastelike consistency, stop the food processor and add the remaining cup of ice water. Stop pureeing once you hear that all of the ice has broken up completely. (For a thinner tahini, add an additional 1 tablespoon plus 2 teaspoons lemon juice and 1 tablespoon plus 2 teaspoons ice water.) Serve immediately or transfer to an airtight container and store in the refrigerator for up to 3 days.

To serve, spread the tahini in a small bowl. Top with the sesame seeds and olive oil and serve with the pita.

Hummus

"Achi bo lenagev hummus!" That's a phrase you'll hear every day throughout Tel Aviv as lunchtime approaches. It translates loosely to, "Brother, let's go wipe hummus," something that in Israel is as much an activity as a meal. Tel Aviv is Israel's capital of hummus, and is home to hundreds of hummuserias, casual cafés where they serve warm plates of fresh hummus and masabacha—a chunkier variation—along with pita and a spread of cold mezze. The very best of all is a little shop in Jaffa called Abu Hassan. It's fucking amazing. People line up all day to get a seat at this place, and then you're in and out in fifteen minutes. The wait is worth it for what, in my opinion, is the best hummus in the world. When I opened Bavel, I told myself, "I'm not putting hummus on the menu if it's not as good as Abu Hassan's." That was my bar, and I think I got pretty close.

The hummus we serve at Bavel is not complicated; it's just about using good ingredients and not adding too much other stuff to compromise that quality. Fresh tahini, high-quality garbanzo beans that aren't too old, fresh garlic, lemon juice, a little bit of cumin—that's it. I use less tahini than you'll find at most places, so you can really taste the garbanzos, and in the end, the hummus is silky, rich, and the closest I'll ever get to having Abu Hassan in Los Angeles.

MAKES 6 CUPS

1 tablespoon plus 2 teaspoons freshly squeezed lemon juice

4 garlic cloves, grated with a Microplane

5 cups Cooked Garbanzo Beans (see right)

1 tablespoon plus 1 teaspoon kosher salt

½ teaspoon ground cumin

½ teaspoon citric acid

1 cup plus 3 tablespoons reserved garbanzo bean cooking liquid from Cooked Garbanzo Beans (see right)

1¼ cups raw tahini paste

¼ cup Tahini (page 67) for serving

1 tablespoon olive oil for serving

1 teaspoon freshly squeezed lemon juice for serving

4 sprigs flat-leaf parsley, leaves picked, for garnish

¼ teaspoon paprika for garnish

To make the hummus: In a small bowl, add the lemon juice and garlic and let sit for 3 minutes.

In a food processor, add the garbanzo beans, the lemon juice and garlic mixture, salt, cumin, and citric acid. Puree this mixture for 5 minutes, stopping once or twice to scrape down the sides of the bowl. Slowly add the garbanzo bean cooking liquid in a steady stream while blending. Continue to blend for another 2 minutes after the liquid has been added. This will aerate the puree so that it becomes light and creamy. Turn the food processor off and add the tahini paste. Blend for 10 seconds; turn off and scrape down the sides of the bowl, then blend for 10 more seconds. Let the hummus sit until it reaches room temperature. Serve immediately or transfer to an airtight container and store in the refrigerator for up to 4 days.

When ready to serve, in a shallow bowl, add ¾ cup of the prepared hummus in a flat layer. Then, while rotating the bowl, use the back of a spoon to spread the hummus up the sides of the bowl to create a large well in the center. Add the tahini to the well and top with the olive oil and lemon juice. Garnish with parsley and paprika.

Cooked Garbanzo Beans

MAKES 8 CUPS COOKED BEANS

3 cups dried garbanzo beans
16½ cups water
2 teaspoons baking soda

Note: For a popular bar snack, drizzle any leftover cooked beans with a little olive oil, season them with salt and a heavy dose of pepper, and eat them with a toothpick alongside a cold beer.

In a large container, add the beans and cover with 6½ cups of the water. Let them soak overnight, between 8 and 16 hours, at room temperature. If your environment is very warm, don't let them soak for more than 8 hours. Soaked beans can be stored in the refrigerator until ready to cook if you aren't ready to use them at the end of the soaking period.

Preheat the oven to 325°F. Drain the beans in a colander and rinse thoroughly.

In a large bowl, add the beans and baking soda and toss to coat. Evenly spread them on a sheet pan and bake for about 8 minutes, until the skins have small blistered lines on them.

In a large pot, combine the remaining 10 cups water and the baked beans. Bring the water to a boil, then decrease the heat to a simmer. While simmering, use a spoon to skim off any foam that has built up on the surface. Simmer for about 50 minutes or until the beans are tender. Turn off the heat and cover the pot and let rest for 15 minutes. Drain the beans in a colander or chinois over a bowl, reserving the cooking liquid. Measure out 5 cups of the cooked garbanzo beans for making Hummus (see left). Reserve the remaining beans for garnish or to make Hummus Masabacha (page 73).

Hummus Masabacha

Masabacha is a thicker, chunkier, more rustic version of hummus that's hand-whipped rather than blended in a food processor, and it probably resembles the kind of hummus that was eaten for centuries before electricity came along. We mash ours with a pestle and serve it on top of our regular hummus, so you get two different textures in each bite.

SERVES 2

¾ cup Hummus (page 70)
½ cup Masabacha (recipe below)
1 tablespoon plus 1 teaspoon olive oil
1 teaspoon freshly squeezed
  lemon juice
2 sprigs flat-leaf parsley, leaves
  picked, for garnish
2 sprigs cilantro, leaves picked,
  for garnish

In a shallow bowl, add the hummus in a flat layer. Then, while rotating the bowl, use the back of a spoon to spread the hummus up the sides of the bowl to create a large well in the center. Add the masabacha in the well of the hummus. Top with the olive oil and lemon juice. Garnish with the parsley and cilantro.

Masabacha

MAKES 4 CUPS

2 large garlic cloves, grated
  with a Microplane
2½ teaspoons kosher salt
¼ cup flat-leaf parsley leaves,
  roughly chopped
3 tablespoons plus ½ teaspoon
  freshly squeezed lemon juice
1 cup raw tahini paste
¾ cup cold water
2½ cups Cooked Garbanzo Beans
  (page 71)

In a stainless-steel bowl, add the garlic, salt, and parsley and, using a pestle, mash to create a chunky paste. Then add the lemon juice and let the mixture marinate for 3 minutes. Add the tahini and water, then, using the pestle, stir vigorously to emulsify for about 1 minute. Then add the cooked garbanzo beans and stir with the pestle to combine. If the mixture is too thick add a little more water. Store in an airtight container for up to 3 days.

Hummus with Tahini & Celery Leaf Chermoula

This chermoula is made from celery leaves, herbs, spices, and a little bit of anchovy, like a salsa verde, to honor my Italian cooking roots. Spoon some over a plate of hummus and tahini for a bright, acidic, super-flavorful dip.

SERVES 2

¾ cup Hummus (page 70)
¼ cup Tahini (page 67)
2 tablespoons Celery Leaf Chermoula (recipe below)
1 tablespoon olive oil

In a shallow bowl, add the hummus in an even layer across the bottom. Then, while rotating the bowl, use the back of a spoon to spread the hummus up the sides of the bowl to create a large well in the center. In the well, add the tahini, then top with the chermoula and oil.

Celery Leaf Chermoula

MAKES ½ CUP

2 large garlic cloves, minced
½ teaspoon kosher salt
5 oil-packed anchovy fillets, drained
1 teaspoon ground cumin
1½ teaspoons ground coriander
1 serrano chile, halved lengthwise and cut into thirds, seeds included
½ cup loosely packed chopped flat-leaf parsley leaves
½ cup loosely packed chopped cilantro leaves
1 cup chopped celery leaves (preferably lighter-colored leaves from the inner ribs)
2 tablespoons freshly squeezed lemon juice
¼ cup plus 1 tablespoon olive oil

In a mortar and pestle, add the garlic, salt, and anchovies and mash until a paste forms. Add the cumin, coriander, and chile and continue to mash. Add the parsley, cilantro, and celery, mashing them in the mortar until a solid green paste forms. Then add the lemon juice and oil and stir to combine. Use immediately. The herbs will oxidize and turn brown after 24 hours.

Hummus with Avocado Tahini & Pepita-Chile Oil

I call this my L.A. hummus. The combination of the subtle avocado and the spicy chile oil—like a deep, dark salsa negra—is as reminiscent of the Middle East as it is of Los Angeles. I use ice water in the tahini to keep it from getting warm while blending, which can make it bitter. The pickled mango has just enough acidity to keep the tahini from turning brown, so it will stay fresh for up to 3 days.

Note: The Pepita-Chile Oil (page 78) is an ambitious recipe, but the result speaks for itself. For a simpler variation, you can use the chile oil we use in our Turkish Eggs (page 145), which will deliver a similar heat.

SERVES 2

¾ cup Hummus (page 70)
¼ cup Avocado Tahini (recipe below)
1 tablespoon Pepita-Chile Oil
  (page 78)
1 tablespoon olive oil
1 teaspoon freshly squeezed
  lime juice
¼ cup loosely packed cilantro
  leaves for garnish

In a shallow bowl, add the hummus in an even layer across the bottom of the bowl. Then, while rotating the bowl, use the back of a spoon to spread the hummus up the sides of the bowl to create a large well in the center. In that well, add the tahini, then top with the chile oil, olive oil, and lime juice. Garnish with the cilantro.

Avocado Tahini

MAKES 1¼ CUPS

1 small avocado, skinned and pitted
½ garlic clove, grated with
  a Microplane
1 teaspoon kosher salt
1 tablespoon plus 1 teaspoon amba
  (pickled mango paste)
¼ cup raw tahini paste
1½ teaspoons freshly squeezed
  lemon juice
¼ cup plus 1 tablespoon ice water

In a food processor, combine the avocado, garlic, salt, mango paste, tahini paste, lemon juice, and water and blend until emulsified into a creamy puree.

Pour the mixture into a fine-mesh sieve or tamis and press through into a bowl until smooth. (If you don't mind some chunks of amba, or pickled mango paste, you can skip this step.) Use immediately or store in the refrigerator in an airtight container for up to 3 days.

CONTINUED

Pepita-Chile Oil

MAKES ABOUT 1¼ CUPS

SPECIAL
EQUIPMENT:

*Candy or other
probe-style
thermometer*

¾ cup grapeseed oil

2 dried morita chiles (may substitute dried chipotle peppers)

1 dried guajillo pepper

2 dried puya peppers

3 dried chiles de árbol

1 star anise

4 green cardamom pods

1 teaspoon ground cumin

½ teaspoon ground coriander

¼ teaspoon ground caraway

3 cloves store-bought pickled Persian garlic,* minced

1 garlic clove, minced

2 teaspoons pickled Persian garlic pickling liquid

¼ cup white sesame seeds

¼ cup pepitas (pumpkin seeds)

You can find jars of pickled Persian garlic (torshi seer) in almost any Middle Eastern market.

Add the oil to a small saucepan fitted with a candy thermometer and bring the temperature to 250°F. Adjust the heat to maintain a temperature between 250°F and 290°F. Add the morita chiles and toast in the oil for 2 to 3 minutes, until they become a deep brown color. Add the dried peppers, star anise, and cardamom pods and cook in the oil for about 2 minutes, until everything turns a dark brown. Remove from the heat and add the cumin, coriander, and caraway to bloom. Then add the garlics, letting them fry off the heat for about 1 minute. Then add the pickled garlic liquid, cover, and set aside for at least 30 minutes or up to 1 hour to infuse.

In a small dry sauté pan over high heat, add the sesame seeds and toast for 1 to 2 minutes, while shaking the pan continuously, until the seeds are golden brown, then remove from the heat and set aside.

In a separate small dry sauté pan, add the pepitas and toast for 2 to 3 minutes, while shaking the pan continuously, until they start to swell and pop. Remove from the heat and set aside.

Remove the cardamom pods and star anise from the infused grapeseed oil and reserve.

Pour the oil mixture into a blender and puree. Then pour the mixture into a small bowl and add the sesame seeds, pepitas, and the reserved star anise and cardamom to the pureed oil. Use immediately or store in an airtight container in the refrigerator for up to 3 months. Bring to room temperature before using.

Yogurt & Labneh

You don't find a lot of dried, aged cheeses in the Middle East; the warm climate just won't allow for it. Instead, though, you have this amazing range of fresh cheeses and cultured dairy products like yogurt and labneh, things that you don't need to hold at a certain temperature for extended periods of time. These rich, tangy spreads are used to marinate and tenderize meat, act as a cooling element in spicier dishes, and are often the centerpiece of a light breakfast or lunch, usually paired with a variety of cool, crunchy salads.

Labneh is just drained yogurt. But where fresh yogurt is creamy and light, labneh is dense, thick, amped up, almost like a cream cheese. Both recipes start the same way, which is by making yogurt. At the restaurant, we make huge amounts in the oven, but at home, the process is incredibly simple, using a yogurt maker or electric pressure cooker. You just need something that can hold a stable, low temperature for six hours or more.

MAKES 2 CUPS

SPECIAL EQUIPMENT:

Dairy or other probe-style thermometer

Yogurt maker or electric pressure cooker (or any insulated container that can hold a heated temperature for at least 6 hours)

Cheesecloth

Kitchen twine

Kitchen scale (for yogurt)

6 cups whole milk
3 tablespoons cultured yogurt*

Add the milk to a large saucepan or Dutch oven fitted with a dairy or probe-style thermometer and warm over low heat. Gently stir the milk with a spatula, scraping the bottom of the pan to prevent scorching, until the milk reaches 120°F. Meanwhile, add the starter to a small bowl.

Once the milk reaches 120°F, add 6 tablespoons of the heated milk to the starter and gently stir to combine. Meanwhile, continue to heat the remaining milk in the saucepan until it reaches 180°F, occasionally stirring with a spatula while gently scraping the bottom and checking the temperature.

Once the milk reaches 180°F, remove the pan from the heat and let the milk cool until it reaches 120°F. Then add the starter mixture and gently stir to combine.

Transfer the mixture to a yogurt maker or electric pressure cooker and incubate for 6 hours at 110°F.

Gather a piece of cheesecloth about 10 inches wide by 16 inches long. Cut the cheesecloth lengthwise, unfold it, then refold it the opposite direction. Prepare three layers of cheesecloth in this way. Nest a fine-mesh strainer or chinois into a large container (bowl or plastic tub) so that it will stay upright without falling over, then line with the layered cheesecloth.

Any store-bought plain yogurt can be used here.

CONTINUED

After 6 hours, pour the incubated yogurt into the prepared strainer. Using kitchen twine, tie up the cheese-cloth into a tight-enough bundle that it forces moisture out of the yogurt.

For Yogurt:

Transfer the cheesecloth bundle to the refrigerator and let drain for 1 hour and 20 minutes. (We recommend reserving the whey, or liquid released from the yogurt, for other uses, like the yogurt sauce with our Turkish Eggs on page 145, or the lovage puree with the Grilled Oyster Mushroom Kebabs on page 129.) Once the yogurt has drained, transfer from the cheesecloth to an airtight container. Store in the refrigerator for up to 3 days.

For Labneh:

To make labneh, which is much thicker in consistency, drain the yogurt** for an additional 40 minutes, or 2 hours total, to remove more of the whey, making it denser. Store in an airtight container in the refrigerator for up to 3 days.

***Option: You can use store-bought yogurt to make labneh; just increase the draining time to 6 hours.*

Farm Cheese

The process to make this thick, creamy spreadable cheese is nearly identical to how you make ricotta. But instead of using buttermilk to trigger the separation of curds and whey, our farm cheese begins with yogurt, which makes the end result even richer, with a great subtle acidic tang. We serve this topped with a little bit of rose za'atar, salt, and olive oil alongside slices of our Buckwheat Sourdough (page 163) for dipping.

MAKES ABOUT 3 CUPS

SPECIAL
EQUIPMENT:

*Dairy or other
probe-style
thermometer*

Cheesecloth

4 cups whole milk

2 cups heavy cream

1 cup Yogurt (page 81); may
substitute store-bought whole
milk Greek yogurt

2½ teaspoons kosher salt

Combine the milk, cream, and yogurt in a saucepan fitted with a dairy thermometer and whisk gently until blended. Place over very low heat and warm, scraping the bottom of the pan with a spatula every 5 minutes or so, until a thick skin forms on top, the solids (the cheese) start separating from the liquid (the whey), and the thermometer reads 208°F, about 30 minutes. Do not let the mixture boil. Remove the pan from the heat and cover tightly with plastic wrap to trap all of the moisture and allow the solids to settle. Let sit for 30 minutes.

Cut a large piece of cheesecloth and fold it to make a piece that is four layers thick and large enough to cover a fine-mesh strainer or chinois. Line the strainer with the cheesecloth and place it over a large pot or bowl. Pour the cheese into the cheesecloth and loosely tie the ends of the cheesecloth over the top to cover. Let the cheese drain for about 4 hours, until it's reached a nice firm consistency.

Transfer the cheese from the cheesecloth to a large bowl, then add the salt and mix until it is evenly distributed. Use immediately or store in an airtight container in the refrigerator for up to 4 days.

Farm Cheese Spread

SERVES 2

½ cup Farm Cheese (recipe above)

1 tablespoon olive oil, plus more
for serving

1 teaspoon Rose Za'atar (page 22)

Pinch of Maldon or other flaky sea salt

Buckwheat Sourdough (page 163)
or store-bought country loaf,
for serving

Kosher salt and freshly ground
black pepper, for serving

Add the farm cheese to the bottom of a small shallow bowl. Using a spoon, spread the cheese across the base of the bowl, creating subtle wells and peaks. Evenly distribute the oil and za'atar across the surface and season with the salt. Lightly toast slices of sourdough, then lightly brush with olive oil, season with salt and pepper, and serve alongside the spread.

Whipped Feta

Good feta cheese is a wonderful thing, but the truth is there's also a lot of really bad feta out there—dry, crumbly, and harshly acidic. Whipping in some crème fraîche transforms even mediocre feta into a creamy, light spread without any of that aggressive chalkiness. Look for feta that is still in the brine. My favorite is Valbreso brand, which you can find in many stores.

MAKES 1½ CUPS

1 cup packed feta cheese, crumbled
½ cup crème fraîche*

We prefer Kendall Farms or Bellwether Farms brand.

In a small bowl, stir together the feta and crème fraîche until evenly combined and the consistency is similar to cottage cheese; do not overmix. Use immediately or store in an airtight container in the refrigerator for up to 3 days.

Baba Ghanoush

Like most home cooks of her era, my grandmother used to make baba ghanoush by charring the eggplant directly over the flame of a gas stove until their skins blistered and the flesh tasted of smoke and chemicals. It's a flavor that has, for me, become oddly comforting—a familiar taste of home. But for everyone else, roasting the eggplant directly over hot coals avoids that harsh, gassy flavor and adds a deep, fragrant smokiness to this classic dip. I like to use Japanese eggplant, because they're the easiest to cook all the way through without drying out or becoming bitter. To lighten it up, I mix in a little crème fraîche along with the tahini and add caramelized diced eggplant and fried curry leaves for texture. At the restaurant, we serve this with Fried Whole-Wheat Pita (page 160), but it's also great with any other good bread.

SERVES 4 TO 6

SPECIAL EQUIPMENT:

Candy or other probe-style thermometer

Eggplant Puree

Three 12-ounce Japanese or Chinese eggplant

2 teaspoons freshly squeezed lemon juice

1½ garlic cloves

2½ teaspoons kosher salt

A few turns of freshly ground black pepper, to taste

5 tablespoons crème fraîche

7 tablespoons plus 1 teaspoon raw tahini paste

Caramelized Eggplant

One 12-ounce Japanese or Chinese eggplant, diced into ½-inch pieces

1 teaspoon kosher salt

4 tablespoons grapeseed oil

4 sprigs thyme

4 garlic cloves, smashed

1½ teaspoons red wine vinegar

Fried Curry Leaf Garnish (page 90) or cilantro leaves for garnish (optional)

Fried Whole-Wheat Pita (page 160) for serving

To make the eggplant puree: In a charcoal grill, light the coals. Once ignited, place the eggplant directly on the coals and cook for 8 to 10 minutes, rotating the eggplant as the skins blister, until they are evenly charred on all sides and the skins are soft. Transfer to a cutting board and let rest for 5 minutes. Then, using gloves or kitchen towels to handle the hot eggplant, cut the tops off and halve lengthwise, making sure not to cut all the way through. Scoop out the flesh and let drain in a fine-mesh strainer over a bowl for about 5 minutes, stirring occasionally to help remove as much moisture as possible. (It's fine if some of the burnt skins remain.)

Pour the lemon juice into a bowl and grate the garlic with a Microplane into the juice. Stir to combine and let sit for 3 minutes.

In a food processor, add 2 cups of the eggplant flesh, the lemon juice and garlic mixture, salt, black pepper, crème fraîche, and tahini paste and puree for 10 seconds. Remove the lid and scrape down the sides of the bowl, then transfer the mixture to a bowl and let sit, uncovered, at room temperature for 30 minutes. Set aside or store in an airtight container in the refrigerator for up to 5 days.

To make the caramelized eggplant: Place the diced eggplant in a bowl, add the salt, and stir or toss to coat. Let sit at room temperature for 1 hour.

CONTINUED

Baba Ghanoush, continued

Line a plate with paper towels and set aside. In a medium-size sauté pan over high heat, add 2 tablespoons of the oil, 2 sprigs of the thyme, and half of the garlic. Cook for 2 minutes to infuse the oil, until the thyme starts to fry. Discard the thyme and garlic. Place half of the eggplant in a single layer on the bottom of the pan. Cook, untouched, on one side, until the eggplant is caramelized and light golden brown, about 2 minutes, then flip to caramelize the other side, about an additional 2 minutes. Transfer the eggplant to the prepared plate. Repeat the process with the remaining eggplant.

Once the second batch of eggplant has completely drained but is still warm, transfer all of the eggplant to a bowl and add the vinegar. Stir to combine, then taste and adjust with salt if needed.

When ready to serve, spread half of the eggplant puree evenly into a bowl; store the remaining puree in the refrigerator for up to 5 days. Top evenly with the caramelized eggplant, then garnish with the curry leaves (if using). Serve with the pita on the side.

Fried Curry Leaf Garnish

Canola oil for frying
20 curry leaves
Kosher salt, to taste

Line a plate with paper towels and set aside. In a small saucepan fitted with a candy thermometer, add a 1-inch layer of oil and bring to 375°F. Add the curry leaves and fry for 20 to 25 seconds. Transfer the leaves to the prepared plate to drain and lightly season with salt.

Foie Gras Halva with Dates & Toasted Sesame

When I was younger, I hated halva, the popular Middle Eastern confection made from tahini. I was more of a Twix bar kind of kid, but today something about the richness reminds me a little of foie gras, an ingredient I ate a lot growing up. Foie gras is one of the few classic delicacies open to those who follow a kosher diet (caviar, lobster, and oysters are all off limits). You'll find skewers of it in almost every kebab shop in Israel. After soccer games, my dad and I would stop for skewers at the market, and he'd always order at least one foie gras as a treat. This dish is a combination of these two very different tastes of my youth, making a smooth foie gras mousse that's paired with a sweet date puree and topped with toasted sesame seeds—a nod to halva's tahini, without any of the bitterness.

SPECIAL EQUIPMENT:

11 by 3-inch terrine mold with lid

Vacuum-seal bag (optional)

Foie Gras Halva

MAKES 4¾ CUPS

12 ounces goose liver

1¼ cups plus 2 tablespoons heavy cream

¼ cup unsalted butter

¼ cup port

2 tablespoons moscato

2 tablespoons pear brandy (may substitute apple brandy or other fruit brandy)

6 eggs

2½ teaspoons kosher salt

¾ teaspoon pink curing salt #1*

*Pink curing salt #1, also known as sodium nitrite, is a curing salt used for short cures that will in the end be cooked. This ingredient helps preserve the color and flavor. It also allows the product to be preserved and kept fresh for a longer period of time.

Preheat the oven to 275°F. Bring the liver to room temperature, then dice into 1-inch cubes. Using a spatula or the back of a large spoon, press the liver through a fine-mesh sieve or tamis over a small bowl and set aside. This is the easiest way to clean the livers because the sieve will collect all of the veins and blood.

In a small saucepan, add the cream and bring to a simmer, then remove from the heat and set aside.

In a separate small sauté pan, melt the butter and set aside.

In another small saucepan, add the port, moscato, and brandy and bring to a boil, then lower to a simmer and cook until the liquid has reduced by half. You'll end up with ¼-cup wine-brandy reduction.

In a blender, combine the liver, cream, eggs, wine-brandy reduction, and kosher and curing salts and puree until the mixture becomes a creamy liquid. Slowly add the melted butter to the blender while mixing to emulsify, then strain through an extra-fine-mesh sieve or a chinois into an 11 by 3-inch terrine mold. Cover with a layer of plastic wrap and then top with the lid of the mold to seal in all of the moisture.

Create a water bath, or bain-marie, by nesting the terrine mold in an oven-safe vessel, such as a 9 by 13-inch baking dish or roasting pan. Boil water in a saucepan or kettle, then pour the water into the larger vessel until the water reaches halfway up the level of the foie gras in the terrine mold.

CONTINUED

Bake for 1 hour and 20 minutes, until the foie gras has a very tight jiggle. If it is still too loose, continue to bake until it reaches the desired texture. Let the terrine rest at room temperature for 30 minutes. Transfer to the refrigerator and cool for at least 3 hours. Once cooled, use a spoon to scrape off the thin layer of browned oxidized liver from the surface and discard.

Transfer the mixture to an airtight container and refrigerate for at least 24 hours or up to 3 days.

An optional step: Before serving, transfer the mixture to a vacuum-seal bag and vacuum seal, then refrigerate. This will make for a dense, creamy texture.

Foie Gras Halva Spread

SERVES 2

20 dates, pitted

⅓ cup Foie Gras Halva (page 92)

¼ teaspoon white sesame seeds, toasted (see page 20)

¼ teaspoon black sesame seeds, toasted (see page 20)

¼ teaspoon Maldon or other flaky sea salt

Buckwheat Sourdough (page 163)

Puree the dates in a food processor, adding small amounts of water if necessary to create a paste. Press the puree through a fine-mesh sieve or tamis into a bowl and set aside. (Note that this will make more date paste than is necessary for this recipe, but it's the minimum amount that will blend properly in a food processor. Spread any leftover puree over buttered toast for an anytime treat.)

Using an offset spatula, spread the foie gras over about two-thirds of the surface of the plate, leaving an empty space to one side. Sprinkle the sesame seeds on top of the foie gras. Then spoon about 1 tablespoon of the date paste into a small ramekin or just a dollop alongside the foie gras. Top with salt and serve with toasted slices of Buckwheat Sourdough.

Chapter 2

Vegetables

When I first moved to Los Angeles, I remember shopping at grocery stores and thinking that all the hype I'd heard about California produce was deeply exaggerated. It wasn't until I started working in restaurants that I discovered local farmers' markets, and that's when my mind was blown. So much of Bavel is inspired by the similarities in climate between L.A. and the Middle East, and that's especially true with the produce. Here we have wonderful versions of eggplant, cucumbers, tomatoes, and all of the other vegetables I was familiar with back home. But then you also have all of this produce native to the Americas, like corn and squash, and because of the huge Asian influence, there are all of these amazing Asian greens and herbs. So basically, L.A. has the best of everything. As a chef, you feel as if it's your duty to find ways to work it all into your menu. So that's what I try to do with the vegetable dishes at Bavel, from salads showcasing heirloom lettuces to side-dish odes to mushrooms, cauliflower, and okra, all with the flavors of the Middle East.

Salads

Note: These salad recipes can be doubled (or in some cases even tripled) if desired, because there is enough vinaigrette left over to make a larger portion of the salad.

The salads themselves at Bavel are pretty simple—usually just one or two elements tossed together. The complexity comes from the vinaigrettes, which are like entire dishes unto themselves. The base of the Chicory Salad (page 116), for example, is really just some endive and lemon zest, but the calamansi vinaigrette layers in four different vinegars and citrus juices, bringing brightness and nuance. The Salanova Butter Lettuce Salad (page 115) is essentially just greens with some cilantro stems and sesame seeds for texture, but the green tahini vinaigrette is jam-packed with an entire salad's worth of fresh herbs and vibrant vinegars and juices. The exception here, of course, is the Mushroom Tabbouleh (page 105), which features almost two-dozen ingredients, including mushrooms, pomegranate seeds, sumac, and garam masala, that transform the ubiquitous bulgur-based side into a powerful centerpiece.

Tomato & Plum with Sumac Vinaigrette

Tomatoes have a nice inherent salinity and minerality, and when you pair them with something sweet and tannic like plums, the two ingredients amplify each other. The sweetness and acidity of the plum enhance the flavor of the tomato, making it taste even riper, like the best tomato you've ever had.

This salad is an interpretation of the many purslane salads you'll find throughout the Middle East that combine crisp purslane with tomatoes, onions, and sometimes a little feta cheese. My take incorporates plums and a pinch of sumac in the vinaigrette that give it an awesome tartness. Then, for balance, there's a floral orange blossom crème fraîche underneath, holding everything together.

I love to layer a thicker element, like yogurt, labneh, or crème fraîche, underneath a salad. It helps hold everything in place, so that when you scoop up a bite, it doesn't all slide away. It also lets you have that creamy element without weighing everything down.

SERVES 2

Orange Blossom Crème Fraîche

1 garlic clove, grated with
   a Microplane
1 tablespoon orange blossom water
½ cup crème fraîche
¼ teaspoon kosher salt

32 cherry tomatoes, halved
1 bunch purslane*
1 sprig savory, leaves picked (may
   substitute oregano or marjoram)
1½ tablespoons plus 1 teaspoon
   Sumac Vinaigrette (page 102)
Pinch of kosher salt
A few turns of freshly ground
   black pepper, to taste
1 plum (not too ripe), pitted and
   sliced into ¼-inch-thick slices
Maldon or other flaky sea salt, to taste
¼ teaspoon ground sumac

*You can find purslane in most
Middle Eastern specialty markets.*

To make the crème fraîche: Add the garlic, orange blossom water, crème fraîche, and salt to a medium bowl and stir to combine. Set aside.

To dress the salad: In another medium bowl, add the tomatoes, purslane, savory, and vinaigrette. Season with the kosher salt and pepper and toss to combine.

When ready to serve, spread 3 tablespoons of the crème fraîche across the bottom of a plate and top with the dressed salad. Evenly scatter the plums on top and finish with an additional teaspoon of the vinaigrette, a bit of the Maldon salt, and the sumac.

CONTINUED

Sumac Vinaigrette

MAKES ABOUT ¾ CUP

2 tablespoons coconut vinegar*
2 tablespoons champagne vinegar
½ teaspoon kosher salt
½ teaspoon granulated sugar
½ teaspoon ground sumac
¼ teaspoon orange blossom water
½ cup olive oil

In a small bowl, combine the coconut and champagne vinegars, salt, sugar, sumac, and orange blossom water. Slowly add the oil in a steady stream while whisking, until the dressing is fully combined and emulsified. Use immediately or store in an airtight container in the refrigerator for up to 5 days.

*Coconut vinegar is made out of the sap from the flowers on coconut trees. It is relatively mild in flavor. It can be purchased online or at any Whole Foods or Asian grocery store.

Mushroom Tabbouleh with Golden Balsamic–Mushroom Vinaigrette

Grain salads are big in the Middle East, and tabbouleh is probably the most famous of all. You'll find two basic types of tabbouleh throughout the region—one that is heavy on herbs; the other is heavy on bulgur. This version is more like the latter, which is popular across Armenia and Turkey. There, they tend to use a fine bulgur, but I love the texture of a coarse-ground cracked bulgur because it acts like a sponge, absorbing whatever flavorings you put with it; in this case, earthy elements like our Super Stock (page 47), mushrooms, and Mushroom Vinegar (page 107). To keep the tabbouleh from getting too muddy, we add pomegranate seeds, Meyer lemon zest, herbs, and sumac, and in the end, you have this very savory salad with little pops of sweetness.

SERVES 8

4 cups Bulgur (page 106)

1 cup roughly chopped Sautéed Oyster Mushrooms (page 106)

½ cup pomegranate seeds*

¼ cup minced red onion

1 cup loosely packed flat-leaf parsley leaves, roughly chopped

¼ cup mint leaves (about 20 leaves), roughly chopped

Zest of 1 Meyer or regular lemon

4 tablespoons plus 1 teaspoon Golden Balsamic Mushroom Vinaigrette (page 107)

2 teaspoons kosher salt

1 tablespoon plus 1 teaspoon ground sumac

2 teaspoons dried rose petals for garnish (optional)

In a large bowl, add the bulgur, mushrooms, pomegranate seeds, onion, parsley, mint, lemon zest, vinaigrette, salt, and sumac and stir to combine. Transfer to a platter or large shallow bowl. Garnish with the rose petals (if using) and serve.

*For an easy way to seed a pomegranate, first fill a bowl with water. Split the fruit in half and hold the pomegranate facedown in your hand. Then, with the handle of a knife or the back of a wooden spoon, knock the seeds out into the bowl of water. The seeds will sink and any membranes will float to the top.

CONTINUED

Bulgur

MAKES ABOUT 4 CUPS

2½ cups Super Stock (page 47);
  may substitute high-quality store-
  bought vegetable stock infused
  with the aromatics from the
  Super Stock recipe

2½ teaspoons kosher salt

1⅔ cups coarse-ground cracked
  bulgur wheat*

In a small saucepan, bring the super stock and salt to a boil. Once it reaches a boil, remove from the heat and add the bulgur. Tightly cover the pot with a lid and let it sit for 30 minutes. Once the bulgur has soaked up all the stock, transfer to the refrigerator to cool down and set aside until using.

When shopping for bulgur, seek out our favorite brand, Sunnyland Mills, which can be purchased online.

Sautéed Oyster Mushrooms

MAKES 1 CUP

1 tablespoon grapeseed oil

4 garlic cloves, smashed

4 sprigs thyme

8 ounces oyster mushrooms

¾ teaspoon kosher salt

A few turns of freshly ground
  black pepper, to taste

Line a plate or sheet pan with paper towels. In a sauté pan, add the oil, garlic, and thyme. Cook to infuse the oil for 2 to 3 minutes. Discard the garlic and thyme. Add the mushrooms, salt, and pepper and sauté until golden brown, 2 to 3 minutes. Drain the mushrooms on the prepared plate. You will need to do this in two batches. Set aside.

Golden Balsamic–Mushroom Vinaigrette

MAKES 1⅓ CUPS

2 tablespoons plus 2 teaspoons
  champagne vinegar
2 tablespoons Mushroom Vinegar
  (recipe below)
½ teaspoon ground sumac
1 teaspoon Garam Masala (page 35)
1 teaspoon kosher salt
½ cup olive oil

In a small bowl, combine the champagne and mushroom vinegars, sumac, garam masala, and salt. Slowly add the oil in a steady stream while whisking, until the dressing is combined and emulsified. Use immediately or store in an airtight container in the refrigerator for up to 5 days.

Mushroom Vinegar

MAKES ABOUT 1¼ CUPS

1¼ cups golden balsamic vinegar
1 tablespoon plus 2 teaspoons
  granulated sugar
½ cup dried mushrooms*

In a small saucepan over high heat, add the vinegar, sugar, and mushrooms and bring to a boil. Remove from the heat and let steep for 1 hour. Strain through a fine-mesh sieve. Use immediately or store in an airtight container at room temperature for up to 3 months.

Any mix of store-bought dried mushrooms will do. Or make your own by dehydrating 8 ounces fresh oyster mushrooms at 110°F in a food dehydrator for 24 hours.

Tomato & Feta with Smoked Harissa

To me, a great tomato is like a steak: you don't want to do too much to it. This salad seems basic—just tomatoes over a creamy feta spread—but the salty, smoky harissa adds another layer of complexity that helps the tomatoes really pop. With a salad that features a single ingredient so prominently, it's especially important that the tomatoes are at their prime—ideally at peak season (late summer to early fall in L.A.) and fresh from a farmers' market. In short, if the tomatoes are great, the dish will be. too.

SERVES 2

½ cup Whipped Feta (page 86)

2 large heirloom tomatoes, diced into 1-inch pieces

Maldon or other flaky sea salt

2 tablespoons Smoked Harissa (recipe below)

2 sprigs cilantro, leaves picked

Spread the whipped feta evenly across the bottom of a medium shallow bowl. Top evenly with the tomatoes, then generously season each piece of tomato with the salt. Finish with the harissa and cilantro.

Smoked Harissa

MAKES 1¼ CUPS

SPECIAL EQUIPMENT:

Candy or other probe-style thermometer

¾ cup grapeseed oil

4 small dried morita chiles (may substitute dried chipotle peppers)

2 dried chiles de árbol

1 cinnamon stick

1 star anise

1 teaspoon ground cumin

½ teaspoon ground coriander

¼ teaspoon ground caraway

4 garlic cloves, minced

2 teaspoons white wine vinegar

4 black garlic cloves*

1 tablespoon light brown sugar

½ teaspoon fish sauce salt** (may substitute kosher salt)

¼ cup shelled sunflower seeds

¼ cup white sesame seeds, toasted (see page 20)

In a small saucepan fitted with a candy thermometer, heat the oil over high heat to 250°F, then decrease the heat to low. Do not let the oil go above 290°F. Add the morita chiles and toast in the oil for 2 to 3 minutes. Once the chiles have turned a deep brown, remove them from the oil and set aside. Add the chiles de árbol, cinnamon stick, and star anise to the same oil and cook for about 2 minutes, until they turn dark brown. Remove the pan from the heat. Add the cumin, coriander, caraway, and minced garlic, letting them fry off the heat for 1 minute until fragrant. Then add the vinegar, black garlic, sugar, and salt and set aside to infuse for at least 30 minutes or preferably overnight.

Meanwhile, roughly chop the moritas into pieces the size of the sunflower seeds and reserve.

In a small dry sauté pan over high heat, add the sunflower seeds and lightly toast, stirring constantly, for about 1 minute, until fragrant and warm throughout. Remove from the heat and set aside.

Once the chile oil has infused completely, remove the cinnamon stick and star anise and reserve. Pour the remaining mixture into a blender and puree until smooth. Transfer to a small bowl and add the chopped moritas, sesame seeds, sunflower seeds, star anise, and cinnamon and stir to combine. Use immediately or store in an airtight container in the refrigerator for up to 3 months. Bring to room temperature before using.

Black garlic is garlic that has been fermented in a humid environment, giving it sweetness and umami that amplifies the sweetness of the tomato. You can find it in many gourmet shops or online.

**Our preferred brand of fish sauce salt is Red Boat.*

Speckled Lettuce Salad with Rose Water Buttermilk Dressing

If I had to pick one recipe in this book for you to make first, it would be this one. It's so unfussy but so unbelievably craveable. The buttermilk vinaigrette is almost like a great ranch dressing with a Middle Eastern hit of rose water and turmeric, and the greens and turnips add a bittersweet crunch. Eat this alone for lunch, or pair it for dinner with something indulgent, like a pile of crispy fried chicken.

SERVES 2

4 ounces whole baby speckled lettuce leaves*

1 small turnip, thinly sliced ⅟₁₆ inch thick on a mandoline (about 16 slices)

1½ tablespoons Rose Water Buttermilk Vinaigrette (recipe below)

Kosher salt, to taste

1 teaspoon Rose Za'atar (page 22); may substitute store-bought za'atar

Add the lettuce and turnip to a large bowl; dress with the vinaigrette and season with salt. Gently mix by hand, lightly folding the leaves and turnips to evenly coat with the vinaigrette. Transfer half of the dressed salad to a cold serving bowl. Season with ½ teaspoon of the za'atar, then add the remaining salad and top with the remaining za'atar. Serve immediately.

Speckled lettuce is a variety of romaine that I particularly like here for its bitterness, texture, and color, but you may substitute baby or regular romaine lettuce.

Rose Water Buttermilk Vinaigrette

MAKES ¾ CUP

1 tablespoon champagne vinegar

½ garlic clove, grated with a Microplane

1 tablespoon plus 2 teaspoons crème fraîche

⅓ cup buttermilk

½ teaspoon kosher salt

¼ teaspoon packed grated fresh turmeric

2 teaspoons rose water

In a bowl, combine the vinegar and garlic. Let sit for 5 minutes. Add the crème fraîche, buttermilk, and salt and whisk to combine. Then add the turmeric and rose water and whisk again to thoroughly incorporate. Serve immediately or store in an airtight container in the refrigerator for up to 5 days.

* Pure Freshly ground
  Spices in Toytinsky
* Ground Coffee
* Delicious Halva!
* Dried fruit inf...

Salanova Butter Lettuce Salad with Green Tahini Vinaigrette

We go through a ton of cilantro at the restaurant, and I'm always looking for ways to use the leftover stems. This classic green salad features tender salanova lettuce, which is wonderfully melt-in-your-mouth, but it needs a little something for texture. Cilantro stems give the salad a nice crunch and intense herby flavor. The dressing here is a play on a green goddess, made with a bunch of fresh herbs and, traditionally, mayonnaise. We use tahini instead as a thickener, as well as a variety of vinegars and fresh citrus juice for complexity. A scattering of black sesame seeds over the top is the perfect finisher.

SERVES 2

4 ounces salanova lettuce leaves (may substitute butter lettuce)
1 large bunch cilantro stems, chopped into 1-inch pieces
2½ tablespoons Green Tahini Vinaigrette (recipe below)
Kosher salt, to taste
½ teaspoon black sesame seeds

In a large bowl, add the lettuce, cilantro, and vinaigrette and season with salt. Gently mix by hand, lightly folding the leaves to evenly coat with the vinaigrette.

Transfer half of the dressed salad to a large bowl. Evenly distribute half of the sesame seeds, then add the remaining salad and top with the remaining sesame seeds. Serve immediately.

Green Tahini Vinaigrette

MAKES ABOUT 1 CUP

⅓ cup packed flat-leaf parsley leaves
½ cup packed spinach
1 sprig tarragon, leaves picked
8 chives
2 oil-packed anchovy fillets, drained
1 garlic clove, grated with a Microplane
1½ teaspoons freshly squeezed regular lemon juice
1½ teaspoons freshly squeezed Meyer lemon juice
1½ teaspoons freshly squeezed lime juice
1½ teaspoons champagne vinegar
½ teaspoon kosher salt
Pinch of freshly ground black pepper
⅓ cup grapeseed oil
¼ cup Tahini (page 67)

In a blender, combine the parsley, spinach, tarragon, chives, anchovies, garlic, both lemon juices, lime juice, vinegar, salt, pepper, oil, and tahini. Start blending on low and gradually increase the speed, until the mixture is combined but flecks of fresh herbs are still visible. Serve immediately or store in an airtight container in the refrigerator for up to 5 days.

Chicory Salad with Calamansi Vinaigrette

There's no actual fruit in this salad, but the Meyer lemon zest, fresh lemon and lime juices, and Calamansi Vinaigrette (recipe below) combine to bring a burst of citrus flavor to the mixture of crunchy chicories. The acidity of the dressing and the bitterness of the endive here are a nice contrast to the duck that we usually serve this salad with, but when topped with some crushed walnuts, it can also be a satisfying lunchtime entrée.

SERVES 2

1 head coraline chicory
   (may substitute endive)
1 head red endive
1 head green endive
Zest of ½ Meyer lemon (may
   substitute regular lemon)
1 tablespoon plus 1 teaspoon
   Calamansi Vinaigrette (recipe below)
Large pinch of kosher salt, or to taste
Freshly ground black pepper, to taste

Separate the leaves of the chicory and both endives and place them in a large bowl, then top with the lemon zest. Add the vinaigrette, salt, and pepper, then gently mix by hand, lightly folding the leaves to evenly coat. Transfer to a large serving plate, layering the endive leaves to form a tower. Serve immediately.

Calamansi Vinaigrette

MAKES ¾ CUP

1 tablespoon freshly squeezed
   lemon juice
1 tablespoon freshly squeezed
   lime juice
1 tablespoon champagne vinegar
1 tablespoon calamansi vinegar*
   (may substitute freshly squeezed
   Meyer lemon juice)
½ small shallot, minced
½ teaspoon kosher salt
Pinch of freshly ground black pepper
3 drops orange blossom oil
½ cup olive oil

In a bowl, combine the lemon juice, lime juice, champagne and calamansi vinegars, and shallot and set aside for 10 minutes. Then add the salt and pepper and stir to combine. Add the orange blossom oil, then slowly add the olive oil in a steady stream while whisking, until the dressing is fully emulsified. Use immediately or store in an airtight container in the refrigerator for up to 5 days.

The brand of calamansi vinegar that we use is Huilerie Beaujolaise.

Moroccan Carrot Salad with Meyer Lemon Yogurt

This simple mix of spiced cooked carrots is a popular mezze throughout Morocco. The classic recipe is delicious but doesn't have much in the way of dimension and texture. The Pepita & White Sesame Dukkah in this version gives the salad some much-needed crunch, and fresh radishes and herbs add even more brightness and complexity. Meyer lemon–spiked yogurt is the creamy base that ties it all together.

SERVES 2

8 cups water

3 tablespoons plus 1 teaspoon kosher salt

3 large carrots, peeled and sliced on a bias into ⅓-inch slices

1 teaspoon ground Kashmiri pepper (may substitute ½ teaspoon ground chile flakes plus ½ teaspoon paprika)

½ teaspoon ground cumin

1 tablespoon champagne vinegar

1 tablespoon golden balsamic vinegar

2 tablespoons olive oil

5 drops orange blossom oil

1½ garlic cloves, grated with a Microplane

¼ cup Meyer Lemon Yogurt (recipe below)

3 tablespoons Pepita & White Sesame Dukkah (page 34)

1 radish, shaved or very thinly sliced

2 sprigs dill, leaves picked

In a large saucepan, bring the water and 3 tablespoons of the salt to a boil. Add the carrots and boil for about 6 minutes, until cooked through.

Line a plate or sheet pan with paper towels. Drain the carrots and then place them in a bowl of ice water and shock for 2 minutes. Transfer the carrots to the prepared plate to dry.

Once the carrots are completely dry, transfer them to a medium bowl along with the pepper, cumin, champagne and golden vinegars, olive oil, orange blossom oil, garlic, and the remaining salt and toss to coat.

Spoon the yogurt onto one side of a plate or shallow bowl and place the carrots alongside. Garnish with the dukkah, radish, and dill. Serve immediately.

Meyer Lemon Yogurt

MAKES 1½ CUPS

1 large garlic clove, grated with a Microplane

1 teaspoon calamansi vinegar (may substitute freshly squeezed Meyer lemon juice)

1 teaspoon kosher salt

1¼ cups Yogurt (page 81); may substitute store-bought whole milk Greek yogurt

Zest of 1 Meyer lemon

1 tablespoon orange blossom water

In a bowl, add the garlic and vinegar. Let sit for a few minutes to marinate. Then add the salt, yogurt, lemon zest, and orange blossom water. Stir to thoroughly combine. Serve immediately or store in an airtight container in the refrigerator for up to 3 days.

Dishes

Over the years, I've made a concerted effort to create a balance between the meat-, seafood-, and produce-centric dishes on my menu. It doesn't take a huge platter of meat in the center of the table to make a meal feel celebratory, and the vibrant vegetable dishes in this section prove that.

Confit Okra with Whipped Feta

Every Friday night, my whole extended family used to get together at my grandmother's house for Shabbat dinner. Most times there were twenty-one of us—eleven kids and ten adults—and somehow she would always manage to have everyone stuffed and happy. There'd be platters of stuffed cabbage leaves and beef braised with onions, and in the summer, you could always expect a dish of okra to be on the table. My grandmother had great instincts and knew how to pick exactly which okra at the market were less sticky and slimy. Then she'd pan-fry them, cover them with a tomato base, and bake them low and slow for a long time.

The okra I serve at Bavel is loosely inspired by my grandmother's but also by a dish that Gino Angelini served at his L.A. restaurant, Angelini Osteria, where I worked for many years. He would confit artichokes in olive oil along with onions and parsley, and in the end, the artichokes tasted like themselves, only amplified. My dish is made with okra and more Middle Eastern aromatics, including mint, cilantro, ginger, and turmeric, but like Gino's artichokes, the flavor of the okra is ultimately intensified. I serve the okra over whipped feta to add a bit of acidity and creaminess to this peak summer dish.

SERVES 4

SPECIAL EQUIPMENT:

Candy or other probe-style thermometer

½ large yellow onion, medium dice

4 green onions, white and light green parts only, sliced

½ cup roughly chopped flat-leaf parsley leaves

¼ cup roughly chopped cilantro leaves

¼ cup (about 20 leaves) roughly chopped mint, plus more for garnish

3 garlic cloves, minced

2 teaspoons ground turmeric

1 teaspoon ground ginger

2 teaspoons ground cumin

1 black lime, pricked all over with a knife

1 pound okra

2½ teaspoons kosher salt

2 cups olive oil

¾ cup Whipped Feta (page 86)

Juice of ¼ lemon

Pinch of Marash pepper (may substitute Aleppo pepper)

Maldon or other flaky sea salt, to taste

In a medium saucepan off the heat, add the diced onion, green onion, parsley, cilantro, mint, garlic, turmeric, ginger, cumin, and lime. Mix to combine. Add the okra to the saucepan in an even layer and season with the kosher salt.

Fit the pan with a candy thermometer and add the oil. (Because the okra is sitting on the bed of onions, herbs, and spices, it won't be completely submerged at first.) Transfer the saucepan to the stovetop on high and heat until the oil comes to a boil, about 5 minutes. When the oil reaches a temperature of 210°F, decrease the heat to a simmer, cover, and continue to cook on low for about 10 minutes. Check for doneness every few minutes until the okra is fork-tender but not too soft. (Exact timing will vary depending on the size and freshness of the okra.) Remove the saucepan from the heat and let it sit, covered, for 5 minutes. (The okra will continue to cook while it sits in the oil off the heat, so be careful of overcooking.) Remove the lid and let cool to room temperature.

When ready to serve, evenly spread the whipped feta on the bottom of a plate. Drain the okra and place on top of the feta in an even layer, piling more okra on top of each layer, almost like a pyramid. Top with the mint, lemon juice, and Marash. Add Maldon salt to taste.

You can use the leftover infused oil for roasting vegetables or any other way you like.

Roasted Cauliflower with Hawaij Chile Sauce & Serrano Crème Fraîche

When I first decided to add this Yemeni-style spice blend to roasted cauliflower, it reminded me of the flavors of aloo gobi, that classic Indian dish of cauliflower and potatoes. I decided to lean into the resemblance, adding even more Indian elements, like Kashmiri pepper, makrut lime, and toasted mustard seeds. The serrano crème fraîche adds a great complementary cooling spice to the hot, crisp florets.

SERVES 4

2 tablespoons grapeseed oil

2 garlic cloves, smashed

2 sprigs thyme

1 large head cauliflower,
   cut into 1-inch florets

1 teaspoon kosher salt

2 tablespoons white wine

½ cup Hawaij Chile Sauce (page 126)

Maldon or other flaky sea salt, to taste

1 cup Serrano Crème Fraîche
   (page 126) for dipping

Preheat the oven to 450°F. In a cast-iron skillet over low heat, add the oil, garlic, and thyme. Cook until the oil has been infused with the garlic, about 2 minutes, then discard the garlic and thyme. Add the cauliflower to the pan in an even layer, then add the salt and toss in the pan. Transfer the pan to the oven and roast for about 18 minutes, flipping the cauliflower halfway through, until the cauliflower is fully caramelized.

Remove the pan from the oven and place on the stove over high heat. Add the wine and cook, scraping the browned bits off the bottom of the pan with a wooden spoon or spatula, until the wine is completely evaporated. Add the chile sauce and toss to coat. Continue to cook until the sauce clings to the florets, then remove from the heat.

Transfer to a large plate or serving platter and season with the Maldon to taste. Serve with a side of the crème fraîche for dipping.

CONTINUED

Hawaij Chile Sauce

MAKES 1¼ CUPS

2 tablespoons grapeseed oil

3 makrut lime leaves, thinly sliced

2 teaspoons yellow mustard seeds

2 garlic cloves, minced

⅔ cup diced yellow onion

2 teaspoons kosher salt

2-inch piece fresh ginger,
   peeled and minced

2-inch piece fresh turmeric,
   peeled and minced

2 teaspoons Hawaij (page 26)

2 teaspoons Kashmiri pepper
   (may substitute hot paprika for
   a milder spice)

½ cup plus 2 tablespoons heavy cream

1 tablespoon granulated sugar

¼ cup juice from canned tomatoes

2 Fresno chiles, minced, seeds included

Add the oil to a small saucepan over medium heat. Then add the lime leaves and mustard seeds and cook until the mustard seeds start to pop. Add the garlic, onion, and salt and cook for 3 to 4 minutes while stirring, until the onion begins to soften and turns translucent. Then add the ginger and turmeric, continuing to cook for another 2 to 3 minutes.

Remove the pan from the heat and add the hawaij and Kashmiri pepper, stirring to combine. Return the pan to the stove, over medium heat, just to bloom the spices, about 30 seconds. Add the cream to the mixture and reduce the heat to low. Bring to a simmer, then add the sugar and tomato juice and stir to combine. Return to a simmer, then remove from the heat and add the chiles. Let the pan sit off the heat for 10 minutes to infuse.

Transfer the mixture to a blender and puree on high, until the sauce is smooth and creamy. Use immediately or store in an airtight container in the refrigerator for up to 3 days.

Serrano Crème Fraîche

MAKES ABOUT 1 CUP

2 garlic cloves, grated

1½ teaspoons serrano chile, seeded,
   grated with a Microplane

1 teaspoon freshly squeezed
   lime juice

1 cup crème fraîche

¾ teaspoon kosher salt

Garnish

Dried orange blossom flowers

Dried marigold flowers

Dried rose petals

Shelled pistachios, roasted
   and chopped

In a small bowl, combine the garlic and chile. Add the lime juice and set aside for 2 to 3 minutes to mellow the garlic. Add the crème fraîche and salt and stir to combine. Use immediately or store in an airtight container in the refrigerator for up to 2 days.

When ready to serve, top the crème fraîche with a garnish of orange blossoms, marigold flowers, rose petals, and pistachios.

Grilled Oyster Mushroom Kebabs with Lovage Puree

When I was twenty-one, I spent six months traveling with friends across South America. We would snowboard all day, party all night, and I'd cook meals for everyone in between. I loved it, and that was one of the first times I remember thinking that I wanted to be a chef. While I was in Argentina, I made friends with some locals, who would sometimes take us for Argentinian barbecue. It would take forever to cook the meat because they kept it far away from the fire, but in the end, the meat was super smoky and juicy—really different from the fast and hot grilling I had been used to.

The first time I tasted this mushroom dish while creating recipes for Bavel, it actually reminded me a lot of the meaty smokiness of Argentinian barbecue. I season the mushrooms with a little sumac and elevate them almost 6 inches away from the heat to cook slowly, absorbing all that great charcoal flavor, and in the end, they're as juicy, smoky, and almost as meaty as tender costillas. I serve them atop a bright puree of lovage, a minerally, almost salty green that tastes like a mix between overgrown parsley and celery leaves—or in colder weather, over stinging nettles—with a little crème fraîche, for a complex, satisfying vegetarian dish.

SERVES 4

1 pound oyster mushrooms

Grapeseed oil for coating

Kosher salt and freshly ground black pepper, to taste

1 teaspoon ground sumac, plus more for dusting

2 tablespoons Lovage Puree (page 130)

Note: Make sure to season the mushrooms only lightly with salt; they shrink a lot when they cook, concentrating the salty flavor. You can always add a bit of finishing salt at the end.

Slice the mushrooms off the cluster, leaving a very small amount of stem intact. Using a metal or soaked wooden skewer, thread the mushrooms through the stem, gill-side down, alternating the tops of the mushrooms from left to right, so they cook evenly. You should end up with two full skewers with about fourteen mushrooms on each.

Brush the mushrooms with a generous amount of oil to coat, making sure to oil the gills. Then lightly season with the salt, pepper, and ½ teaspoon of the sumac per skewer.

Preheat a charcoal grill to medium heat (see Grilling Guide on page 192).

Place the mushrooms directly on the grill and cook, flipping the skewers every 2 minutes, for 8 to 14 minutes total, until the edges start to curl and brown, the mushrooms have shrunk significantly, and the stems are soft to the touch. The water will drip from the mushrooms onto the coals to create the smoke that will give them that smoky flavor.

When ready to serve, spread the lovage puree evenly over the center of a plate. Lightly dust the puree with the sumac and place the mushroom skewers on top.

CONTINUED

Lovage Puree

MAKES ABOUT ½ CUP

8 cups plus 3 tablespoons water

2 cups loosely packed lovage,
leaves picked

4 cups packed spinach

2-inch piece fresh turmeric, peeled,
grated with a Microplane

1 garlic clove, grated with a
Microplane

1 teaspoon kosher salt

⅓ cup crème fraîche

½ cup Yogurt Whey (page 81)

1 teaspoon ground cardamom

Bring 8 cups of the water to a boil in a large pot and fill a large bowl with ice water. Blanch the lovage in the boiling water for 2 minutes, then add the spinach and blanch for an additional 2 minutes. Using tongs, remove the greens from the pot and place in the ice water to shock for 2 to 3 minutes, until they are cool enough to handle. Using a colander or fine-mesh sieve, drain the greens, removing any ice. Using your hands, form the greens into a ball, squeezing out as much water as possible. Then place the squeezed greens in a kitchen towel. Wring out the kitchen towel until you remove as much liquid as possible and the greens are almost completely dry.

Place the greens in a blender and add the turmeric, garlic, salt, crème fraîche, whey, cardamom, and the remaining 3 tablespoons water. Mix on high speed, stopping to scrape down the sides when necessary, until the mixture is smooth. If the mixture won't fully blend, add a little more water.

Falafel

Green falafel is made with garbanzo beans and just a ton of fresh herbs. While growing up, I used to get it for lunch at least once a week, often from my dad's favorite childhood spot, called Falafel Palm Ami near central Tel Aviv, and while we don't serve falafel at Bavel, I do make it at home once in a while. I like my falafel to be so creamy and moist that it's almost too juicy to hold its shape, with a bit of texture from small chunks of garbanzos and herbs. I achieve this by balancing the amount of moisture-releasing ingredients in the batter—using fewer yellow onions and more green onions and herb stems—so I don't need to add any additional flour to hold everything together. Then I run everything through a meat grinder to preserve the rustic texture. In the end, these crisp falafel are reminiscent of Spanish croquettes and are best eaten fresh out of the fryer, stuffed into warm pita or dipped straight into a mix of crème fraîche and pickled mango.

MAKES 50 TO 60 FALAFEL

SPECIAL EQUIPMENT:

Meat grinder attachment for stand mixer (You can use a food processor, but the texture will be slightly different.)

Candy or other probe-style thermometer

3 cups dried garbanzo beans

6⅓ cups water

2 cups roughly chopped cilantro with stems, loosely packed

3 cups loosely packed roughly chopped flat-leaf parsley leaves, with stems

6 sprigs dill, roughly chopped, with stems

9 green onions, roughly chopped

½ yellow onion, quartered

1½ teaspoons ground cumin

2¼ teaspoons ground coriander

2 tablespoons plus 1 teaspoon jalapeño powder (may substitute 2 whole fresh jalapeños, chopped, seeds included)

2 teaspoons whole cumin seeds, toasted

2 teaspoons whole coriander seeds, toasted

1 tablespoon plus 2 teaspoons kosher salt

2 teaspoons baking soda

Canola oil for frying

Whole-Wheat Pita (page 157) for serving, optional

Falafel Dipping Sauce (recipe below) for serving

In a large bowl, add the garbanzo beans and cover with the water. Let soak overnight, then drain the beans in a colander and rinse thoroughly. Return the beans to the bowl along with the cilantro, parsley, dill, green onions, yellow onion, ground cumin, ground coriander, and jalapeño powder.

Attach a meat grinder with the ¼-inch die to a stand mixer. Pass the garbanzo bean mixture through the meat grinder into medium bowl. Repeat the process, passing the mixture through the meat grinder a second time. Add the whole cumin, coriander seeds, salt, and baking soda and gently fold to combine; do not overmix.

In a large stockpot fitted with a candy thermometer or a fryer, pour the oil to a depth of 3 inches and heat to 350°F. Line a large plate with paper towels.

Using two spoons, form the falafel mixture into a smooth oval shape with pointed ends; this is called a quenelle. Working in batches, gently drop the quenelles into the oil. Fry for about 2 minutes total, turning with a small-mesh strainer or a spider, until evenly golden brown on all sides. Transfer the falafel to the prepared plate to drain. Serve them in a pita or on their own with the dipping sauce on the side.

Falafel Dipping Sauce

MAKES 1½ CUPS

1 cup crème fraîche

½ cup amba (pickled mango paste)

In a small bowl, stir together the crème fraîche and mango paste until evenly combined. Serve immediately.

Wedding Rice

Traditional Middle Eastern wedding feasts typically revolve around some meaty centerpiece—maybe roast lamb or goat—with a whole spread of dishes, including at least one festive rice dish. Also called jeweled rice, this fragrant Persian-style wedding rice is often studded with all kinds of nuts and dried fruit and is intensely aromatic, cooked with cinnamon and cardamom and finished with fresh dill. When Genevieve and I were married in 2010—in a small ceremony at La Terza, the Los Angeles restaurant where we first met—we had lasagna. If we ever have a redo, we'll serve this instead.

SERVES 4 TO 6

24 green cardamom pods

2 cinnamon sticks

2 tablespoons grapeseed oil

1½ cups diced yellow onion

1½ fresh bay leaves or 1 dry bay leaf

1 tablespoon plus ½ teaspoon kosher salt

2 cups jasmine rice

2 cups water

3 tablespoons unsalted butter

¼ cup packed dill, leaves picked and roughly chopped

1 cup golden raisins

Garnish

Dried rose petals

1 bunch dill, leaves picked

Dried marigold flowers (optional)

Dried orange blossoms (optional)

Preheat the oven to 325°F. Place the cardamom pods and cinnamon sticks on a small sheet pan and toast in the oven for 5 minutes. Remove and set aside.

In a medium saucepan over high heat, add the oil and onion. Tear the bay leaves to release their aroma, then add to the pan. Add 1¾ teaspoons of the salt and sauté for about 3 minutes, until the onion is translucent.

Add the rice to the pan and stir until well coated with the oil. Then add the water, cinnamon sticks, cardamom pods, and the remaining 1¾ teaspoons salt and stir to combine. Bring to a boil, then decrease the heat to medium-low, cover tightly with a lid, and cook for 18 minutes, until the grains of rice are tender and no longer al dente.

Remove the pan from the heat. Uncover and add the butter, dill, and raisins to the top of the rice. Cover the pot again and set aside to rest for another 5 minutes. Remove the lid and fluff with a fork, then cover and let rest for 12 more minutes. Transfer to a large platter for serving and garnish with the rose petals and dill and with the marigold flowers and orange blossoms (if using). Be mindful of the cinnamon sticks and cardamom pods while eating the rice.

Rice Cake

Every time my grandmother would have us over, she would make a baked rice cake, which is sometimes called a tahdig, topped with a simple stew of braised okra. Her version began by lining a nonstick pan with sliced potatoes, then adding in an egg and oil mixture that puffed up around the rice while it baked, making the cake fluffy and sturdy at the same time.

My rice cake has a lot more in common with an Italian saffron risotto than my grandmother's rice cake—it skips the potatoes, uses butter instead of oil, and infuses the egg mixture with saffron, turmeric, and Parmigiano-Reggiano. But in the end, the process is no more difficult than hers, and the final effect when unmolded is just as dramatic.

SERVES 8 TO 10

12½ cups water
¾ cup plus 1 tablespoon plus
  3 teaspoons kosher salt
60 threads saffron
2 cups basmati rice
1 teaspoon ground turmeric
1 cup crème fraîche
½ cup unsalted butter, melted,
  plus more for coating
2 eggs
1 cup packed grated
  Parmesan cheese

Preheat the oven to 400°F. In a large saucepan over high heat, bring the water to a boil. Add ¾ cup plus 1 tablespoon plus 1 teaspoon of the salt. Place the saffron in a small bowl, then scoop out 2 tablespoons of the boiling water from the pot and pour over the saffron threads. Set aside.

Meanwhile, rinse the rice thoroughly in a colander until the water runs clear. Add the rinsed rice to the pot of boiling water and cook, uncovered, for 6 minutes. Using the colander, drain the rice, then rinse under cold water until the rice has cooled down, about 30 seconds.

In a large bowl, combine the turmeric, crème fraîche, butter, the remaining 2 teaspoons salt, eggs, Parmesan, and bloomed saffron along with the blooming water. Stir to combine, then gently fold in the rice and let sit for 10 minutes.

Lightly coat an 8-inch nonstick frying pan with a small amount of butter. Add the rice mixture to the pan and cover with aluminum foil. Bake in the oven for 1 hour.

Remove the rice from the oven, uncover, and let rest in the pan for 10 minutes. Using a plate that is slightly larger than the size of the pan, turn the plate upside down and cover the pan. Use your hand to stabilize the plate from the center and carefully flip the pan, so that it is now on top of the plate. Carefully lift the pan to check if the rice has formed a golden crust. If the crust isn't golden, flip the pan back over, remove the plate, and cook on the stove over low heat for 2 to 4 minutes. Turn out onto the plate once more and slice to serve. Refrigerate any leftovers for up to 3 days and warm before serving.

Chapter 3

Breakfast

I never used to be a morning person—most days I'd wake up late, around 11:00 a.m., craving something substantial like shakshuka or crisp-edged Turkish eggs. Today, as a father and business owner, I'm on a slightly different schedule. I wake up early, go on a run, and come back in time to cook my daughter something nutritious before she heads to school. For me, breakfast these days looks more like a bowl of tangy yogurt with honey, nuts, and seeds, or a toasted slab of buckwheat bread spread with something creamy—stuff to keep me going without weighing me down. Our original plan for Bavel was to be open during the day and serve dishes that satisfied both early and late risers. While we never did get brunch off the ground, the recipes in this chapter are, for now, the next best thing.

Buckwheat Toast with Clotted Cream, Honey & Urfa Pepper

I make a peach dessert at Bestia that uses clotted cream, and it's so popular that we put it on the menu every summer. Clotted cream is the thickened top layer that forms when cream is heated low and slow for several hours. Ori has always loved it—he likes anything with concentrated flavors—and though it's not cultured, clotted cream has a dense, umami-like quality similar to cheese or butter. Ori used to grab some cookies from my pastry station, slather on some of my clotted cream and maybe a little date puree, and eat it as a snack. One day, he said, "What if I put something like this on the menu but on buckwheat toast with some date puree or honey?" It was delicious, but ultimately, he decided it was better as an at-home snack or for breakfast. Here, the Urfa pepper provides an extra sharpness to offset the rich, fatty cream.

—Genevieve

SERVES 4

Four ½-inch-thick slices Buckwheat Sourdough (page 163)
5 tablespoons plus 1 teaspoon Clotted Cream (recipe below)
4 teaspoons honey
1 teaspoon Urfa pepper
Maldon or other flaky sea salt for garnish

Toast the bread and let cool for 1 to 2 minutes. Spread 1 tablespoon plus 1 teaspoon of the clotted cream over each slice and drizzle each with 1 teaspoon honey. Finish each slice with ¼ teaspoon of the pepper and a pinch of salt.

Clotted Cream

MAKES ABOUT 3 CUPS

8 cups unpasteurized or lightly pasteurized heavy cream (do not use ultra-pasteurized; it will not clot)

Preheat the oven to 180°F. Pour the cream into a 9 by 13-inch baking dish (or as close to that size as possible). Place the dish, uncovered, on the middle rack of the oven and bake for 12 hours—overnight is easiest because of the following steps. After exactly 12 hours, gently remove the dish from the oven, being careful not to agitate the cream. Then cover the dish with plastic wrap and refrigerate for 7½ to 8 hours. (Do not let it sit for more than 8 hours or the firm layer will start to dissolve back into the wet layer.) After the cream is set, a layer of thick butterlike cream will have formed at the top. Run a spatula or knife around one edge and tilt the pan to drain the underlying liquid and discard. Scoop out the remaining clotted cream and use immediately or store in an airtight container in the refrigerator for up to 3 days.

Pistachio Nigella Labneh (The Ori Breakfast)

When our daughter, Saffron, was a baby, she had to have yogurt every single day—it was her favorite thing to eat. We went to England with her when she was about one, and I found this quaint little country store with beautiful cheeses, butter, and this really rich, creamy locally made yogurt. It was delicious—Saffron loved it—and every day during our trip, I went to the store to get Saffron a giant jar. On our last day, we bought a small jar to take home on the airplane, and when Ori tasted it, he was floored. It was that yogurt that Ori used as his starter for our homemade yogurt and labneh. We began eating it in the morning, when—especially as a working parent—you're always rushing and don't really have time to make yourself something healthy. Ori would often just quickly take some labneh and top it with chopped pistachios, a drizzle of honey, and—because he was at the height of his nigella seed obsession—a sprinkle of those, too. He used to make a quick one for himself, and then one day, I said, "Hey, make me one!" It was so good. When we were working on this cookbook, I told him that we should feature this recipe—*the Ori breakfast*—and he agreed. It's something that's healthy and sustaining, and unlike oatmeal or eggs, it doesn't require cooking. And while we love the combination of pistachios and nigella seeds, you can top it with whatever nuts and seeds you have on hand.

—Genevieve

SERVES 1

½ cup Labneh (page 81); may substitute store-bought whole milk Greek yogurt, drained in a cheesecloth-lined fine-mesh sieve)
1 tablespoon shelled pistachios
½ teaspoon nigella seeds
1 tablespoon honey

In a medium bowl, spread the labneh in an even layer. Top with the pistachios and nigella seeds and drizzle with the honey.

Turkish Eggs

The chile oil is the real magic of this recipe—a spicy condiment that's good on almost anything and keeps for weeks. I especially like it drizzled over fried eggs, as in this quick dish that was inspired by a breakfast I once had in Turkey, where the eggs were cooked in yogurt. Here, two sunny-side up eggs get covered with a cool, tangy yogurt sauce and a bit of that fiery chile oil. Just break the yolks and it all comes together—a hit of sour, spicy, salty, and creamy flavors, perfect for sopping up with a piece of toasted bread.

SERVES 2

SPECIAL EQUIPMENT:

Candy or other probe-style thermometer

Vegetable oil for frying
8 sage leaves
Kosher salt, to taste
1 tablespoon unsalted butter
2 eggs
Heaping ¼ teaspoon Maldon or other flaky sea salt
2½ tablespoons Yogurt Sauce (page 146)
1 teaspoon Chile Oil (page 146)

Line a plate with paper towels. In a medium saucepan fitted with a candy thermometer, pour a 1-inch layer of vegetable oil and heat to 375°F. Add the sage leaves and fry for 20 seconds. Transfer to the prepared plate to drain and season immediately with the kosher salt.

In a nonstick frying pan over high heat, melt the butter and cook until the milk solids start to slightly brown, 1 to 1½ minutes. Remove the pan from the heat and crack the eggs directly into the pan. Then return the pan to the stove over high heat. Add the Maldon salt to the top of the egg yolks and fry the eggs until the bottoms just start to brown and the whites are just set, 2 to 2½ minutes. If the bottoms start to brown before the whites are set, decrease the heat to low and continue to cook for another 1 to 2 minutes. Then remove the pan from the heat and, using a spoon, baste the egg whites with the brown butter.

Transfer the eggs to a serving plate and drizzle with any remaining brown butter. Top with the yogurt sauce, chile oil, and sage leaves for garnish.

CONTINUED

Yogurt Sauce

MAKES ½ CUP

¼ cup plus 2 tablespoons Yogurt
   (page 81); may substitute store-
   bought whole milk Greek yogurt*

¼ cup crème fraîche

1 teaspoon freshly squeezed
   lemon juice

½ teaspoon kosher salt

1 garlic clove, grated with
   a Microplane

2 tablespoons Yogurt Whey (page 81)

In a small bowl, add the yogurt, crème fraîche, lemon juice, salt, garlic, and whey and gently stir with a spatula to combine. Use immediately or store in an airtight container in the refrigerator for up to 5 days.

If using store-bought yogurt and it is too thick, thin it with 1 to 2 tablespoons water.

Chile Oil

MAKES ABOUT 1¼ CUPS

SPECIAL
EQUIPMENT:

*Candy or other
probe-style
thermometer*

½ cup grapeseed oil

½ cup olive oil

1 cinnamon stick

1 fresh bay leaf

3 whole cloves

3 green cardamom pods

2 garlic cloves, halved lengthwise

1-inch piece fresh turmeric,
   peeled and thinly sliced

¼ cup plus 1 tablespoon ground
   chile flakes

2 tablespoons paprika

½ teaspoon kosher salt

In a small saucepan fitted with a candy thermometer, add the grapeseed and olive oils, followed by the cinnamon stick, bay leaf, cloves, cardamom, garlic, and turmeric. Heat the oil over medium heat to 225°F. Remove from heat and let sit to infuse for 10 minutes.

Add the chile flakes, paprika, and salt and let cool to room temperature. Transfer to an airtight container and refrigerator for 24 hours before using. (This will allow the oil to thicken up.)

When ready to use, remove from the refrigerator and stir to combine, making sure to fully incorporate any solids that settled to the bottom. The oil can be stored in an airtight container at room temperature for up to 3 months. When using, avoid the large whole spices, like cardamom, cloves, cinnamon stick, and bay leaf. Serve over fish or anything else you would like to give a little extra heat to.

Shakshuka

Shakshuka isn't really a breakfast dish; it's a brunch dish—the kind of rich, potent thing you devour with friends around 11:00 a.m. or noon, when you finally crawl out of bed after a long night of partying. Or at least that's how I remember eating it as a teen in Tel Aviv. Back then, I would go out crazy late, sleep in even later, and when I finally woke up, my dad would greet me with a big pan of shakshuka.

Like so many other dishes, my favorite shakshuka is my dad's, an idealized version of the standard recipe—eggs cooked in a saucy base of tomatoes, bell peppers, onions, garlic, and cumin. Mine is an amplified version of that, with peppers that are dehydrated to up their intensity and a little red zhoug.

SERVES 1 OR 2

1 tablespoon grapeseed oil
1 garlic clove, thinly sliced
½ small yellow onion, julienned
¼ teaspoon ground cumin
½ teaspoon ground coriander
¾ cup juice from canned tomatoes
1½ dried bell peppers,* julienned
½ teaspoon kosher salt
½ cup water
2 to 3 tablespoons Red Zhoug
    (page 41), to taste**
2 eggs
Maldon or other flaky sea salt, to taste
1 teaspoon olive oil
10 flat-leaf parsley leaves for garnish
10 mint leaves for garnish

In an 8-inch cast-iron or other heavy skillet over high heat, add the grapeseed oil and garlic. When the garlic starts to sizzle, add the onion, stirring frequently so they don't burn. Once the onion starts to brown, add the cumin and coriander. Stir to coat and let the spices bloom until fragrant. Add the tomato juice, dehydrated pepper, kosher salt, water, and zhoug and stir to combine. Bring the mixture to a boil, then decrease the heat to a simmer. Gently crack each egg directly into the pan with the sauce and top each yolk with a small pinch of the Maldon salt. Cook for 4 to 6 minutes, until the tomato sauce thickens, then decrease the heat to low. Cook for 1 to 2 more minutes, until the whites are set but the yolks still have some jiggle.

Remove the pan from the heat and drizzle with the olive oil. Garnish with the parsley and mint leaves and finish with more Maldon salt to taste. Serve straight out of the cast-iron pan.

*For dried bell peppers, quarter 1 whole red bell pepper and dehydrate at 110°F for 24 hours. You can substitute fresh bell pepper for the dried in this recipe, but the flavor will be slightly muted.

**For less spice, use only 2 tablespoons zhoug.

Chapter 4

Breads

Bread is a crucial element of any meal in the Middle East—equal part side dish and utensil for scooping up the array of salads, dips, and meats that make up a proper Middle Eastern feast. There are hundreds of distinct regional varieties, ranging from flatbreads like pita and laffa to leavened, laminated, and enriched loaves. At my house, it was almost always my dad's bread at the center of the table—he'd make his own from scratch using all kinds of grains and flours. He actually owned a bakery for a few years, selling Jerusalem bagels, baguettes, and other loaves.

Although beautiful breads are now becoming increasingly abundant across L.A., back when I opened Bestia in 2012, this was not so much the case. Most of the commercially made bread you got then was dry or tough, and I recognized that I was going to have to make my own. So, I started experimenting with bread at home. The first version I ever made was the Tartine loaf, and from there, it was all about trial and error, failing a million times and trying to understand why. Eventually, I learned to predict things— how much gluten would make a bread tough versus chewy, how to knead and tie to get the exact crumb and shape I wanted. I learned how to care for a sourdough starter, how to manipulate texture with different flours, and how the high heat of a wood oven can help with rise and crust. But it was the Bestia pizza dough that really tortured me; developing that recipe took years off my life but eventually taught me the hard way how to manipulate flour and water. Since then, making bread has become a passion of mine.

I'm really proud of all of the breads we serve at Bavel, and a lot of that is due to all of those hours spent perfecting the bread at Bestia. There, we use a wood oven, but that means the oven is off-limits to everything else during the middle of the day. Since I originally planned to serve lunch at Bavel, I wanted to come up with a loaf that could be made in a conventional oven; that is how I developed our buckwheat sourdough. My pita bread is used for dipping, not stuffing, so I knew I could focus on making something really moist and tender. Laffa is an Iraqi flatbread that's traditionally used for tearing and swiping through food. Here, we encourage diners to use it as a utensil for pinching off hunks of meat from our lamb neck shawarma. Malawach is a rich breakfast staple back home, layered with butter and flattened, almost like a crushed croissant.

The techniques behind each of these breads are not difficult, but they do take some practice. Don't be discouraged if the loaf doesn't come out perfect the first time. As I said, bread making is all about trial and error, but I've worked hard to make sure these recipes are as error-proof as possible.

Flours

Our baked goods—from the breads here to the pastries and cakes in Desserts (page 237)—call for a range of flours, all of which are used for one reason or another, from gluten content to flavor. While most breads will work with all-purpose flour, these recipes are designed for the specific characteristics of each flour, and I encourage you to familiarize yourself with the incredible variety in texture and taste you can achieve with alternative flours. Our preferred store-bought flour brand is King Arthur. Also, bread is one place where weight measurements are essential for consistent results. A small digital scale is an inexpensive investment for a lifetime of precise cooking.

- **AP Flour:** AP, or all-purpose, flour is literally all-purpose. You can use it for practically anything. It has a medium gluten percentage, which means you can generally make both cakes and bread from it just fine. You just need to knead it a lot longer for bread and be very gentle with it for more delicate baked goods. It is neutral in flavor, so it can be used in almost any recipe.

- **Whole-Wheat Flour:** This is a less-refined wheat flour with the germ still attached, which provides a nice nuttiness. I use this when I want to give something added flavor. In almost any recipe, swapping a bit of whole-wheat flour for all-purpose flour will add dimension, not to mention fiber and protein. But whole-wheat flour can dry out your dough, so be careful and adjust the moisture accordingly.

- **Buckwheat:** Buckwheat is not actually wheat—or a grain for that matter—it's a seed, which means there is no gluten in it. I like the bitter, smoky element it adds to bread, but more importantly, it can lower the total gluten of a recipe. That's why our Buckwheat Sourdough (page 163) is almost custardy—it has protein and structure but is very tender and almost cakey because of the buckwheat.

- **Bread Flour:** Bread flour is a high-gluten, high-protein flour that helps give the structure needed for a good loaf, especially if a dough has any oil or fat in it, which inhibits gluten.

- **Einkorn:** Einkorn is an heirloom wheat that's low in gluten. It adds flavor, much like a whole wheat, but with a lower gluten content. The taste is smooth and almost chocolatey, and Genevieve uses it in a lot of cakes to add flavor and keep a tender crumb.

- **Cake Flour:** Cake flour is also low in gluten, so it's great for cakes, but it has a neutral flavor, which is good for something where you want the other ingredients to shine through.

- **Sonora Wheat:** Whenever I want the flour itself to add to the flavor profile of a recipe, I use Sonora wheat. Sonora wheat is a very sweet, golden nutty flour (think graham crackers) and has the same gluten content as all-purpose pastry flour. It can be hard to find, though. We're lucky to have a local farmer in the L.A. area who grows it and a small local miller who grinds it fresh, but you can also purchase it online.

Sourdough Starter

This sourdough starter is a flavorful natural leavening agent for our Buckwheat Sourdough (page 163) and Whole-Wheat Pita (page 157). You can use the discarded starter after each feed for sourdough pancakes—just substitute 10 to 20 percent of the flour and water in a standard pancake recipe with the same volume of starter to add a nice tang.

SPECIAL
EQUIPMENT:

*Instant-read
thermometer*

Starter

¾ cup bread flour
2 tablespoons buckwheat flour
½ cup water

Feeding the Starter

3 cups bread flour
1½ cups water

Make the starter: In a large bowl, add the bread flour and the buckwheat flour. Stir with a whisk to combine.

In a medium bowl, add the bread and buckwheat flour mix with the water. Using your hands or a spatula, mix until thoroughly combined and free of any dry bits. Cover with a kitchen towel or plastic wrap. Let sit at room temperature (70°F or warmer) for up to 3 days, until small bubbles form around the edges; this indicates fermentation. By this point, it should smell a little funky and have a tart taste.

A thin crust will form on the top of the starter. Peel off that layer of crust and discard, then store in an airtight container in the refrigerator. When you are ready to use the starter, begin the 3-day feeding process.

To feed the starter: In a clean medium bowl, add ¼ cup of the starter. Then add 1 cup of the bread flour and ½ cup of the water. Using your hands or a spatula, mix to combine. It will resemble a pancake batter at this point. Cover with a kitchen towel and let sit at room temperature for 24 hours. Repeat this feeding process once every 24 hours at the same time of day for the next 3 days. Each time, transfer ¼ cup of the starter to a clean bowl, discarding the remainder. Then add 1 cup bread flour and ½ cup water. Cover and let sit at room temperature. The fermentation will cause the batter to rise and fall consistently after a few days of feeding.

After the 3-day period, test the starter to see if it is ready to use. Fill a small bowl with water. Drop a small piece of the starter into the water. If the piece of starter floats, it is ready to use. If it doesn't float, but seems active (you can see bubbles), wait another 1 to 2 hours and then repeat the float test.

This starter can be stored in the freezer in an airtight container. When ready to use, thaw and repeat the 3-day feeding process.

Whole-Wheat Pita

Back in the early days of Bestia, I was asked to appear on an episode of Munchies' *Chef's Night Out*, a Vice show where a bunch of chefs and other food industry professionals run around town drinking and eating together. They asked me to make a dish that would be good for everyone at the very end of the night, and I realized that even though I was working as a chef at an Italian restaurant, I didn't really know what drunk Italians eat. I definitely knew what my drunk friends back in the Middle East eat, though, so I decided to make a classic falafel using my dad's recipe to stuff inside some fresh-baked pita. I had never made pita before, but I quickly came up with a basic recipe, and it was perfect on the very first try. I swear, as soon I had made it, I turned to Genevieve, who was pregnant at the time, and said, "We need to open a Middle Eastern restaurant." That pita was the real start of Bavel.

Note: This recipe is not exactly the same as the version we serve at Bavel. That one uses whole eggs and requires temperatures higher than what is possible in a home oven to rise properly. This version uses egg whites, and cooks up perfectly on a pizza stone in any home oven. I never like to say that any recipe is foolproof, but this one is pretty close.

MAKES 18 PITA

SPECIAL EQUIPMENT:

Pizza stone

Instant-read thermometer

Yeast Mixture

1 teaspoon (4g) active dry yeast
¼ cup (60g) water (110°F)
2 teaspoons (7g) granulated sugar

Dough

1 cup (240g) room temperature water
6 (170g) egg whites
1 cup (200g) Sourdough Starter*;
   may substitute 7 tablespoons (100g)
   water plus ¾ cup plus 3 tablespoons
   (100g) bread flour
6½ cups (750g) bread flour
1¼ cups (150g) whole-wheat flour
2 tablespoons plus 1 teaspoon (21g)
   kosher salt
2 tablespoons (34g) honey
¼ cup plus 2 tablespoons (85g)
   olive oil
¼ cup plus 2 tablespoons (85g)
   canola oil

To activate the yeast: In a bowl, whisk together the yeast, water, and sugar and let sit for 10 minutes to bloom the yeast, or until the yeast starts to float and begins to bubble.

To make the dough: In a stand mixer fitted with the dough hook attachment, add the water, egg whites, yeast mixture, sourdough starter, bread and whole-wheat flours, salt, and honey. Mix on medium-low for 2 minutes and 40 seconds, then first add the olive oil, followed by the canola oil, in a slow, steady stream. Mix for a total of 10 minutes. Then cover the mixer bowl with a kitchen towel or plastic wrap and let sit for 1 hour to let rise. (Note that the volume of the dough will not change significantly.)

On a lightly floured surface, turn out the dough and separate into eighteen equal portions (100g each). Shape the dough on the work surface by cupping your hand over one portion of dough and rolling in

The sourdough starter here is optional, but using it will give the bread a deeper flavor and longer shelf life.

CONTINUED

a counterclockwise motion, using the friction of the work surface to create a smooth round ball. Place the dough portions 2 inches apart on a flour-dusted sheet pan. Cover with plastic wrap and refrigerate for 24 to 48 hours. (Note that the longer the dough is resting, the more flavor it will develop.)

Preheat the oven to 500° to 550°F or the oven's highest temperature setting. Place a pizza stone in the oven.

When you are ready to bake, remove the dough from the refrigerator and bring to room temperature, 30 to 45 minutes. Generously dust your work surface with flour. Then, using a bread spatula or bench scraper, gently lift the dough from the container and place onto the work surface. Dust the dough with flour on both sides.

Using a rolling pin, roll up and back once, then give the dough a quarter turn. Roll up and back again and give a quarter turn once more. Repeat the process two more times for a total of four times, until the dough is between ⅛ and ¼ inch thick and about 6 inches wide. (Lightly toss the dough rounds from hand to hand to remove any excess flour.)

Using a pizza peel, inverted sheet pan, or even your hands, slide the pita dough onto the preheated pizza stone. Close the oven door and bake for 1½ to 3 minutes, until the pita puffs up and the top of the dough separates from the bottom. Remove the dough from the oven and let the bread rest for 2 to 3 minutes before serving. Repeat with the remaining dough rounds.

Freeze unused pita in an airtight container or a ziplock bag for up to 1 month; to reheat, thaw in the microwave for 25 seconds, then preheat a cast-iron skillet and cook quickly on both sides until heated through.

Fried Whole-Wheat Pita

Traditionally, pita gets baked in the oven or grilled over an open flame. Frying the pita provides a more delicate donutlike texture and is the perfect pairing for the tangy baba ghanoush.

SERVES 2

SPECIAL EQUIPMENT:

Candy or other probe-style thermometer

Canola oil for frying
1 to 3 shaped pieces Whole-Wheat Pita (page 157)
Pinch of Maldon or other flaky sea salt
Baba Ghanoush (page 88) for dipping

Line a plate or sheet pan with paper towels. Add 2 inches of oil to a large saucepan fitted with a candy thermometer and heat over high heat to 375°F. Add the pita, one at a time, to the oil and fry for about 45 seconds, using a spoon to baste the top of the pita. Once the pita just starts to plump, flip and fry on the other side for about 45 seconds more. Continue to baste the top with oil. When the pita rises to the top, use a slotted spoon to remove the pita from the oil and let it drain on the prepared plate to rest for about 3 minutes. Then put the pita back into the oil and fry for another 45 seconds, again basting the top and flipping about halfway through, until it plumps up. If the pita tears, just flip it to fry on the side that isn't torn so no oil gets inside of the pita. Remove the pita from the oil with a slotted spoon and let it drain on the prepared plate. Immediately season with the salt while still hot. Repeat with the remaining pita. Serve right away with the baba ghanoush.

Buckwheat Sourdough

My original vision for Bavel included lunch service, which meant the wood oven would be too busy during the day to bake bread. I needed a great loaf that could cook in a conventional oven; that is how this buckwheat sourdough loaf came to be—and it has since become one of Bavel's signature items. The dough is still kneaded by hand and folded, much like the rustic loaf we serve at Bestia, but these loaves get baked in sealed loaf pans so that all of the steam is contained, resulting in great lift and a caramelized but still chewy crust. The technique might look complicated, but this is really a pretty easy bread. Even if your ties and kneads aren't precise, it's not a big deal. Just cut it, shape it, throw it in the pan, and it will cook perfectly.

Today it comes sliced and toasted alongside our Farm Cheese (page 84). I also love it with the Baba Ghanoush (page 88), Foie Gras Halva (page 92), or just spread with a little clotted cream or butter. This loaf stays fresh for a really long time—just leave it on the counter wrapped in plastic, and even after slicing, it will stay fresh for almost a week.

Note: It's important to use a young starter, within 4 hours after the last feed. This will ensure that the bread is not too acidic.

MAKES 2 LOAVES

SPECIAL EQUIPMENT:

Two 13 x 4-inch Pullman loaf pans

Instant-read thermometer

3¼ cups (770g) filtered water (93°F)

1 cup (200g) Sourdough Starter (page 154)

7⅓ cups (850g) bread flour

1 cup (100g) whole-wheat flour

½ cup (50g) buckwheat flour

2 tablespoons plus 1 teaspoon (21g) kosher salt

1½ teaspoons unsalted butter for greasing the pans

2½ tablespoons (20g) black sesame seeds

Test the starter to see if it is ready to use (see page 154). In another large bowl, add the bread, whole-wheat, and buckwheat flours and whisk to combine.

Add the starter to the bowl with the warm water, followed by the flour mixture. Then, using your hands, squeeze the flour, making sure to push it in between your fingers to mix out any lumps, scraping the sides of the bowl as needed to fully incorporate all of the dry ingredients. Mix like this for a total of about 3 minutes, until no lumps remain.

Cover the bowl with a kitchen towel or plastic wrap and let sit for 30 minutes. Evenly sprinkle the salt over the dough, then dip your hands in water to prevent sticking and knead the salt into the dough by hand, again squeezing the dough through your fingers to thoroughly incorporate, 2 to 3 minutes, until the salt is completely dissolved. Scrape any excess dough from your fingers or from the sides of the bowl back into the dough mass.

CONTINUED

Buckwheat Sourdough, continued

We use Pullman loaf pans at the restaurant; they can be found online.

Cover the bowl again with a kitchen towel or plastic wrap. Let sit for 3½ hours, folding every 30 minutes by pulling all four corners of the dough mass toward the middle and pinching together. Then repeat the process again, pulling the four corners of the smaller mass toward the middle and pinching together once more.

After the final 30 minutes, turn the dough out onto a lightly floured work surface. Lightly dust the top with flour. Divide the dough into two even portions (about 950g per portion). Pull one portion of dough toward you, rolling it onto itself five or six times, turning 90 degrees with every roll, until you have a tight round ball. Repeat with the second dough portion, then let sit both balls on the work surface, uncovered, for 30 minutes.

Meanwhile, butter all sides and the bottoms of two 13 by 4-inch Pullman loaf pans, using ¾ teaspoon per loaf pan.

Using a bench scraper, flip over one portion of dough. Imagining the dough like a rectangle, take the top two corners farthest from you, fold them toward each other in the center, and pinch to "tie." Do the same to the bottom two corners. Then rotate the dough 90 degrees and repeat the process with the new top and bottom corners. Then, with the dough in the same position, tie again three times, pulling from the top corners, the middle, and the bottom. Rotate 90 degrees and tie three times once again. Flip the dough so it is

seam-side down and shape by pulling the mass toward you once to roll it onto itself. Repeat this rolling process three more times, rotating the dough 90 degrees each time you roll, until you have turned the dough a full 360 degrees. Repeat the tying and shaping processes for the second dough portion.

Place the sesame seeds in a large bowl. Dip each dough portion into the seeds and sprinkle more seeds over the top to coat the dough on all sides. Transfer the dough to the prepared pans, with the seam-side down. Cover the pans with a lid or aluminum foil and refrigerate for 8 to 16 hours.

Remove the pans from the refrigerator and let sit, covered, at room temperature for 30 to 60 minutes, until the center portion of the dough has risen to about 1 inch below the rim of the pan. Preheat the oven to 500°F.

Bake the covered loaves for 10 minutes. Decrease the oven temperature to 450°F and bake for 10 minutes more. Then decrease the oven temperature to 400°F, uncover, and bake for 14 to 20 more minutes, until the loaves are golden brown. Remove the pans from the oven, immediately place the loaves on a wire rack, and let cool for at least 1 to 1½ hours before slicing.

Wrap in plastic wrap and store at room temperature for up to 5 days or freeze for up to 1 month. Bring to room temperature before slicing.

Malawach with Tomato Sauce & Dill Crème Fraîche

Imagine a flaky croissant that's been flattened, pan-fried, and served with all sorts of sweet or savory spreads. This is the essence of malawach—a delicious, rich Yemeni flatbread that essentially sustained me through most of my many teenage stoner years.

I had never made malawach from scratch before opening Bavel. My first few attempts to make it were fine, but with all-purpose flour, it was difficult to form without the dough tearing. So, I added a little einkorn flour for stability; this also reduced the amount of gluten, allowing the malawach to be both flaky and crispy at the same time.

You can serve these with almost anything, but I like them best with a bit of our tomato sauce, a cooling dill crème fraîche sauce, and a dollop of spicy Strawberry Zhoug. A 6-minute soft-boiled egg is also a good accompaniment.

Note: Every step listed here is crucial to properly stretching the dough—especially the resting periods. If you don't let the dough rest between steps, it won't relax and will tear when you try to form it.

MAKES 10 MALAWACH

1¾ cups (400g) unsalted butter, softened to room temperature, plus more for greasing

6¾ cups (780g) all-purpose flour

2 cups (220g) einkorn flour

1½ tablespoons (18g) granulated sugar

2 tablespoons plus 1½ teaspoons (22g) kosher salt

1 teaspoon (5g) baking powder

2⅔ cups (620g) water

Dill Crème Fraîche (page 171) for serving

Tomato Sauce (page 171) for serving

Strawberry Zhoug (page 42) for serving

Olive oil for drizzling

Lightly butter a large bowl and sheet pan. In a stand mixer fitted with the dough hook attachment, combine the all-purpose and einkorn flours, sugar, salt, baking powder, and water and mix on medium speed until a dough forms. Transfer the dough to the prepared bowl, cover with a kitchen towel or plastic wrap, and let rest for 30 minutes.

Lightly butter a cool, clean work surface and turn the dough out onto it. Divide the dough into ten equal portions (about 162g per portion). Place on the prepared sheet pan, cover with a kitchen towel or plastic wrap, and let rest for 30 minutes.

Reapply butter to your work surface, roll one portion of the dough into a 9-inch round* and set aside. Repeat the process with the remaining nine portions and let rest for 2 minutes.

Then, one at a time, stretch each round by hand into an 18 by 24-inch paper-thin rectangle. Some tears are okay. Measure out 40g of butter, then take half of that (20g) and pat and spread evenly with your fingers over the stretched dough. Fold the two long sides of the rectangle inward 3 inches and pat a little of the remaining butter on top of each folded layer. Repeat the folding and buttering four times total, until you close the dough like a book and have one single long strip of dough about 3 inches wide by 24 inches long. Butter the top of that long strip with the remaining butter. Then, working from the bottom, fold upward in 3-inch increments, until you have a squarelike mound of dough. Repeat the entire process with the remaining dough rounds and butter.

Transfer all of the portions back to the sheet pan, cover with plastic wrap, and refrigerate for at least 1 hour until the butter is solidified.

Meanwhile, cut twenty pieces of parchment paper into 12-inch squares. Then remove the dough from the fridge and line a clean work surface with a piece of parchment paper. Place one portion of dough on top and pat down the top with another piece of parchment. Using a rolling pin, roll the dough, rotating 45 degrees with each roll, into a 9-inch round.* Repeat with the remaining portions. Stack and store in the

CONTINUED

Malawach with Tomato Sauce & Dill Crème Fraîche, continued

freezer, still sandwiched between the parchment and then wrapped in plastic wrap.

When ready to cook, place one frozen dough round into a cold 12-inch sauté pan (or any size pan that has a bottom surface that is 9 inches or larger), then place the pan over very high heat. Cook until the butter starts to release, the middle begins to soften, and the malawach turns golden brown, about 90 seconds. Flip and cook on the other side for another 90 seconds. Flip again and cook for 45 seconds. Flip again and cook for 15 seconds. Flip one last time and cook for 15 more seconds. Remove from the heat and let rest for 30 seconds. Transfer to a cutting board and slice into four equal slices.

Serve one hot malawach alongside a small dish containing 3 tablespoons crème fraîche, 3 tablespoons tomato sauce, 2 teaspoons strawberry zhoug, and a drizzle of olive oil.

CONTINUED

Dill Crème Fraîche

MAKES 1¼ CUPS

2 garlic cloves, grated with
   a Microplane

1½ teaspoons serrano chile, seeds
   removed, grated with a Microplane

1 teaspoon freshly squeezed
   lime juice

1 cup crème fraîche

2 tablespoons plus 1 teaspoon
   packed dill leaves, roughly chopped

¾ teaspoon kosher salt

In a small bowl, combine the garlic, chile, and lime juice and let sit for 2 to 3 minutes to mellow the harshness of the garlic. Then add the crème fraîche, dill, and salt. Stir to combine. Store in an airtight container in the refrigerator for up to 2 days.

Tomato Sauce

MAKES ABOUT 1 CUP

2 to 3 large tomatoes

2 sprigs thyme

Peel of ½ lemon

½ teaspoon granulated sugar

¾ teaspoon kosher salt

2 tablespoons olive oil

A few turns of freshly ground
   black pepper, to taste

Grate the tomatoes over a box grater, using the largest holes on the grater; discard the skins. You need 1 cup grated tomatoes.

Using a fine-mesh sieve over a bowl, drain the grated tomatoes for 1 to 2 minutes, shaking the sieve often to remove any excess liquid.

Rub the thyme between your palms to gently bruise the leaves and release the oils. In a bowl, add the drained tomatoes, lemon peel, sugar, salt, thyme, oil, and pepper. Mix to combine. Let sit to infuse for 30 minutes. Remove the lemon peel and thyme stems (any leaves of thyme that remain are fine) before serving.

Laffa

While we were still in the early stages of planning Bavel, I invited one of the world's top laffa oven builders to come to L.A. Laffa is a traditional Iraqi flatbread, similar to a pita but with no pocket, and it's made in a special tandoor-type drum oven called a tabun. We flew this guy out and put him up for a full week. While together, he and I built a giant round oven made out of metal, clay, brick, mortar, and concrete. The final tabun was enormous—the size of a large pizza oven. But after we finally found a restaurant space and began to design the Bavel kitchen, we realized that we couldn't fit both a tabun and a wood-burning oven, which was indisputably more versatile. So, after all of that, I had to abandon my tabun, and to this day it's just been sitting in the parking lot at Bestia.

Laffa isn't typically something you make yourself; rather, it's something you buy fresh at a kebab shop, where it's someone's entire job to bake laffa nonstop. You slide the meat off the skewer using the piping-hot laffa, then you soak the laffa in the meat juices, swipe it through some tahini, use it to pick up a chunk of meat, and eat it just like that. While I may not have a tabun at the restaurant, I developed a recipe that results in tender, flavorful laffa, even when made in a conventional oven. They are great on their own or topped with a little bit of our Mushroom Za'atar (page 25) and olive oil before baking (see Variation, page 174).

Note: This recipe calls for three different flours, the combination of which makes a low-gluten dough that allows the edges to get crispy but the interior to remain supple.

MAKES 12 LAFFA

SPECIAL EQUIPMENT:

Pizza stone

2¾ cups (650g) room temperature water

½ teaspoon (1g) active dry yeast

2 teaspoons (5g) baking powder

⅓ cup (40g) Sonora wheat flour

¾ cup plus 2 tablespoons (100g) einkorn flour

7½ cups (860g) all-purpose flour, plus more for dusting

2 tablespoons plus 1 teaspoon (21g) kosher salt

2 tablespoons plus ½ teaspoon (27g) granulated sugar

¼ cup (50g) olive oil, plus 1 teaspoon for coating

Semolina flour for dusting the pizza peel

½ cup olive oil and 3 teaspoons Maldon or other flaky sea salt for topping

Add the water to the bowl of a stand mixer fitted with the dough hook attachment, then add the yeast, baking powder, Sonora flour, einkorn flour, all-purpose flour, salt, and sugar. Mix on low speed for 2 minutes and 40 seconds, then slowly stream in ¼ cup (50g) of the oil while the mixer is still running. If the oil causes the dough to slide, increase the speed for 5 seconds to incorporate it quickly, then decrease the speed to low. Continue to mix for another 3 minutes and 20 seconds.

Coat a medium bowl with 1 teaspoon of the oil. Using a scraper, transfer the dough from the stand mixer bowl to the oiled bowl. Cover with a kitchen towel or plastic wrap and let sit for 30 minutes.

Lightly dust a work surface with all-purpose flour. Turn the dough out onto the surface and begin to knead by pulling the top of the dough over the mound toward yourself, tucking it underneath, then pushing the dough away from you with the heels of your hands. Turn the

CONTINUED

Laffa, continued

dough 90 degrees and repeat the pull-push knead once more. Repeat this process twice more, until you have completely rotated the dough 360 degrees.

Divide the dough into twelve equal portions (about 142g per portion) and let them rest, uncovered, for 5 minutes. Take one portion and, using your fingers, pull the dough toward you to roll the dough onto itself. Turn 90 degrees and repeat the shaping motion. Repeat this process twice more, until you have completely rotated the dough 360 degrees and it forms a smooth ball. Repeat with the remaining portions.

Lightly dust the bottom of a sheet pan or baking dish with all-purpose flour. Add the dough balls and cover with a lid or plastic wrap and store in the refrigerator for 72 hours.

When ready to bake, preheat the oven to 500° to 550°F or the oven's highest temperature setting. Place a pizza stone in the oven.

Remove the dough from the refrigerator and let it sit at room temperature for an hour before stretching. Lightly dust a pizza peel or inverted sheet pan with semolina flour and set aside. Lightly dust the dough in the container with all-purpose flour, then turn one portion out onto a floured work surface. Using a rolling pin, flatten the dough into an oval about 12 inches long. Pick it up with your hands and, using your knuckles, stretch it lengthwise into a slightly longer and wider oval.

Place the stretched dough onto the prepared pizza peel or inverted sheet pan. Top with 2 teaspoons of the oil and ¼ teaspoon of the Maldon salt. Slide the dough onto the preheated pizza stone and bake for 3 minutes. Remove from the oven and transfer the flatbread to a serving platter. Repeat the rolling and baking process for the remaining portions. Serve immediately while hot.

Variation: Mushroom Za'atar Flatbread: Top the stretched dough with 1 tablespoon Mushroom Za'atar (page 25) and 1 tablespoon olive oil in an even layer, then finish with Maldon salt. Bake at 500°F for 4 minutes. Remove from the oven and transfer to a serving platter. Serve immediately while hot.

Chapter 5

Seafood

Though much of the Middle East is famous for its coastline, the cuisines of the region aren't as seafood-centric as you might think. The staple dishes are largely meat, grain, or vegetable based, and seafood shows up mostly in simple preparations, like a piece of fish that's grilled or fried with lemon, salt, and pepper. In North African countries, you'll find a number of dishes where small fish get braised with tomatoes, bell peppers, and cumin. But suffice it to say the seafood dishes I serve at Bavel are more inspired by my own tastes and by the types of ingredients I have access to in Los Angeles than by any traditional Middle Eastern preparation. From there, I weave the flavor profiles of the region into each recipe, from fresh scallop crudo with mint and pomegranate seeds (page 182) to flaky grilled dourade smothered in crispy whole-seed chermoula (page 187).

Harissa Prawns with Zucchini Tzatziki

Morita chiles are smoked Fresno chiles, and they give a deep smoky heat to the harissa marinade on these delicious spicy prawns. There are also anchovies and fish sauce for umami, orange zest for brightness, and a little sugar and honey to help the spice mixture caramelize on the grill. The final dish, one of our favorite things on our menu, has a bit of everything: acid, smoke, sweetness, spice, bitterness from the char, and a cooling creaminess from the tzatziki served alongside. Pick up a prawn with your hands, drag it through the tzatziki, eat the meat, suck the head, lick your fingers, and go back for more.

SERVES 2 TO 4

4 dried morita chiles (may substitute dried chipotle)

3 large dried California chiles, seeded

1 large red bell pepper, stemmed, seeded, and quartered

4 Fresno chiles, stemmed

Zest of 1 orange

1 tablespoon freshly squeezed orange juice

8 garlic cloves, grated with a Microplane

1 teaspoon tomato paste

1 tablespoon plus 2 teaspoons fish sauce

4 oil-packed anchovy fillets, drained

1 tablespoon honey

½ cup loosely packed brown sugar

½ teaspoon paprika

2 teaspoons ground cumin

1 teaspoon ground caraway

1 teaspoon ground coriander

1 tablespoon plus ½ teaspoon kosher salt

¼ cup plus 1 tablespoon grapeseed oil, plus more for grilling

2 tablespoons olive oil

2¼ pounds (1 kg) whole prawns,* shells removed, heads and tails intact

Zucchini Tzatziki (page 181) for serving (optional)

Fresh mint, dill, and Meyer lemon juice for garnish

Place the morita and California chiles in a small heatproof bowl. Bring a kettle or small saucepan of water to a boil and pour over the chiles, submerging them. Cover the bowl with plastic wrap and let sit for 10 minutes.

In a blender, combine the bell pepper, Fresno chiles, soaked dried peppers, orange zest and juice, garlic, tomato paste, fish sauce, anchovies, honey, sugar, paprika, cumin, caraway, coriander, and salt.

In another bowl, combine the grapeseed and olive oils.

Slowly puree the pepper and chile mixture on medium speed, then stream in the oil mixture while mixing. Blend until smooth and thoroughly combined.

Place the prawns into a large bowl. Wearing gloves, thoroughly coat the prawns on all sides with the pepper puree. Cover the bowl and marinate the prawns for 8 to 24 hours in the refrigerator. (Do not marinate for any longer than 24 hours or the prawns will start to cure.)

Preheat a charcoal or gas grill (see Grilling Guide on page 192). Remove the prawns from the refrigerator and lightly coat with grapeseed oil. Grill the prawns over medium heat until the marinade caramelizes onto the prawns and the color darkens, about 2 to 3 minutes, then flip and repeat on the other side. This should take 4 to 6 minutes total, depending on the size of the prawns.

Transfer the prawns to a serving bowl. Serve with a bowl of tzatziki on the side (if using). Garnish with the mint and dill and a small squeeze of lemon juice.

We use New Caledonian blue prawns at Bavel. They feed on kelp, which gives them a vibrant blue color when raw, and when cooked, they turn a deep red-orange. You can use any good-quality prawns or large shrimp.

CONTINUED

Zucchini Tzatziki

MAKES 1½ CUPS

Four 5-ounce zucchini, tops and bottoms trimmed

2½ teaspoons kosher salt

2 teaspoons freshly squeezed lemon juice

1½ garlic cloves, grated with a Microplane

½ cup crème fraîche

½ cup Labneh (page 81); may substitute store-bought whole milk Greek yogurt, drained

⅛ teaspoon mint powder

Note: This cooling dip makes a great cold appetizer on its own, garnished with a few mint leaves, some fresh dill, and drizzled with a bit of olive oil or served as a spread with grilled bread.

Using a mandoline, slice the zucchini into rings about ¹⁄₁₆ inch thick. Transfer the zucchini to a large bowl, add 2 teaspoons of the salt, and toss to coat. Let sit for 5 minutes, then gently massage the zucchini by hand to help release the moisture. Cover and let sit for 1 more hour, then scoop the zucchini into a dish towel and squeeze out as much of the liquid as possible. Transfer 1½ cups of the squeezed zucchini to a separate bowl.

In a small bowl, combine the lemon juice and garlic and let sit for 3 minutes, then add to the squeezed zucchini. Add the crème fraîche and labneh and stir to combine. Finally, add the mint powder and the remaining ½ teaspoon salt and stir to combine. Use immediately or store in a covered container in the refrigerator for up to 3 days.

Scallop Crudo with Burnt Serrano Oil

There are a few dishes on our menu that reflect more of L.A.'s Latin American influence than anything in the Middle East, and this crudo is one of them. With diced raw scallops in citrus juice spiked with burnt serrano chiles, this crudo has all the spicy refreshment of an aguachile, while the pomegranate reduction, torn mint, and black sesame seeds are nods to the flavors of the Middle East.

SERVES 2 TO 4

1 small Persian cucumber

8 ounces sushi-grade scallops, diced into ½-inch cubes

½ teaspoon gray sea salt (may substitute any high-quality coarse sea salt)

1 tablespoon Burnt Serrano Oil (page 184)

6 tablespoons Citrus Mix (page 184)

6 mint leaves, torn

16 cilantro leaves, torn

1 teaspoon black sesame seeds, toasted (see page 20)

Seeds from ½ pomegranate for topping

Place the cucumber directly over the burner of a gas stove (alternatively, char with a kitchen torch or over the flames of a charcoal or gas grill) until the skin is evenly charred. Transfer the cucumber to the refrigerator and chill until cool, about 10 minutes. Cut the charred cucumber in half lengthwise and then slice crosswise into ¼-inch-thick half-moons. Meanwhile, place a small bowl for serving in the freezer to chill.

In a small bowl, add the scallops, salt, and serrano oil and gently mix with a spoon to coat the scallops, making sure not to overmix. Add the scallops to the chilled serving bowl and top with the charred cucumber slices. Add the citrus mix by gently pouring along the edge of the bowl so it runs to the bottom but doesn't tint the scallops.

When ready to serve, top with the mint, cilantro, sesame seeds, and pomegranate seeds.

CONTINUED

Burnt Serrano Oil

MAKES ABOUT 1 CUP

7 serrano chiles
⅔ cup grapeseed oil

Place the chiles directly over the burner of a gas stove (alternatively, char with a kitchen torch) until the skins are evenly charred on all sides. Transfer the chiles to the freezer for 10 minutes to cool down. Once cool, add the chiles and oil to a blender and mix on low for about 10 seconds. Increase the speed to high and blend for 45 seconds, until the chiles and the oil have emulsified. Transfer the chile oil to a bowl and set aside until serving or store in an airtight container in the refrigerator for up to 5 days. The leftover chile oil can be used to add an extra kick to any dish you like.

Citrus Mix

MAKES ABOUT 1 CUP

½ cup pomegranate juice
2 tablespoons freshly squeezed orange juice
3 tablespoons freshly squeezed Meyer lemon juice (may substitute 2 tablespoons regular lemon juice plus 1 tablespoon water)
3 tablespoons freshly squeezed lime juice
½ teaspoon kosher salt
2 teaspoons granulated sugar

In a small saucepan over medium heat, bring the pomegranate juice to a boil, then decrease the heat to low and simmer until the volume is reduced by half. Remove the pan from the heat and set aside until cool, then refrigerate until chilled, 15 to 20 minutes.

Fill a large bowl with ice and nest a smaller bowl in it. Add the liquids to the small bowl in the following order: reduced pomegranate juice, orange juice, lemon juice, and finally the lime juice. Add the salt and sugar and whisk until dissolved. Strain the liquid through a fine-mesh strainer into another small bowl. Nest the bowl of strained liquid in the large bowl of ice and refrigerate. Any leftover juice can be used for a vinaigrette or in a cocktail.

Grilled Dourade with Whole-Seed Chermoula

Dourade (also called sea bream, or in Italian, orata) is one of my favorite fish. It's wonderfully flavorful, by which I mean that it does taste a bit fishy. Some people like their fish to taste like nothing, but I like mine to taste of the sea: clean, fresh, and yes, a little fishy. The natural oils in dourade are what make it so perfect for grilling, helping to keep it moist even when the heat fluctuates. Here, the delicate fish is butterflied and quickly grilled over charcoal on both sides to infuse it with a subtle smoke flavor. Then we smother the crispy skin with a whole-seed chermoula that's full of texture and flavors like ginger, turmeric, and mushroom. I highly recommend making a big batch of this chermoula and keeping it on hand as a condiment for just about anything.

SERVES 2

1 pound whole dourade*
2 teaspoons kosher salt
6 turns of freshly ground black pepper
Olive or grapeseed oil for greasing
  the grill rack
1½ tablespoons Whole-Seed
  Chermoula (page 188)
Juice of ¼ lime
1 turnip, thinly sliced
2 sprigs cilantro, leaves picked

*Ask your fishmonger to butcher the dourade as follows: deboned, butterflied, head attached but split (see photo).

Season the inside of the fish with 1 teaspoon of the salt and 3 turns of the pepper. Flip and season the skin side with the remaining 1 teaspoon salt and another 3 turns of the pepper.

Preheat a charcoal or gas grill to medium heat (see Grilling Guide on page 192). Brush the rack with a light coating of oil to prevent the fish from sticking.

Using tongs, lift the fish by the tail and gently drape it, skin-side down, starting with the head, onto the grill. Grill over medium heat for about 3 to 4 minutes, until about half of the flesh has turned opaque. If the fish curls at all while cooking, press it down so it lies flat. Flip the fish flesh-side down by grabbing the tail with tongs and gently lifting the fish off the grill with a spatula, and cook for another 1 to 2 minutes, until the fish is opaque throughout.

Carefully transfer the fish to a serving plate skin-side up. Spread an even layer of the chermoula over the skin. Garnish with the lime juice, turnip, and cilantro.

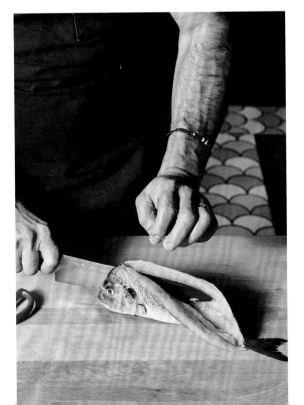

CONTINUED

187

Whole-Seed Chermoula

MAKES 1 CUP

2 teaspoons oyster mushroom powder (may substitute any mixture of store-bought dried mushrooms, ground to a powder)

1 teaspoon kosher salt

1 tablespoon granulated sugar

1 teaspoon ground ginger

½ teaspoon ground turmeric

1½ teaspoons Urfa pepper (may substitute ground chile flakes)

½ teaspoon freshly ground black pepper

½ cup grapeseed oil

6 garlic cloves, minced

2 tablespoons minced shallots

1 tablespoon plus ½ teaspoon whole fennel seeds

1 tablespoon whole cumin seeds

1 tablespoon plus 2 teaspoons whole coriander seeds

2 tablespoons white wine vinegar

In a small heatproof bowl, add the mushroom powder, salt, sugar, ginger, turmeric, Urfa pepper, and black pepper and stir to combine.

Set a fine-mesh strainer over a small saucepan and set aside.

In a separate small saucepan over high heat, add the oil and garlic. When the garlic starts to sizzle, decrease the heat to low and continue to cook, stirring occasionally to prevent burning, for 2 to 3 minutes, until golden and crispy. Pour the garlic mixture into the fine-mesh strainer, reserving the garlic-infused oil in the pan. Add the fried garlic to the bowl of ground spices. Wipe the saucepan clean of any oil or remaining garlic and set the fine-mesh strainer over it.

Place the saucepan containing the garlic-infused oil over high heat, then add the shallots. Once the shallots start to sizzle, decrease the heat to low and continue to cook, stirring occasionally to prevent burning, for 2 to 3 minutes, until golden and crispy. Pour the shallot mixture into the fine-mesh strainer, reserving the oil in the saucepan. Add the fried shallots to the bowl of spices and fried garlic.

Add the fennel, cumin, and coriander seeds to the saucepan with the shallot- and garlic-infused oil and place over high heat. When the seeds start to sizzle, decrease the heat to low and continue to fry for 2 minutes.

Remove the pan from the heat. Then, while stirring continuously, pour the fried seeds and hot oil into the bowl with the spices in small batches. Stir until thoroughly mixed, and then add the white wine vinegar.

Let the mixture cool. Use immediately or store in an airtight container in the refrigerator for up to 3 months. Bring to room temperature before serving.

Chapter 6

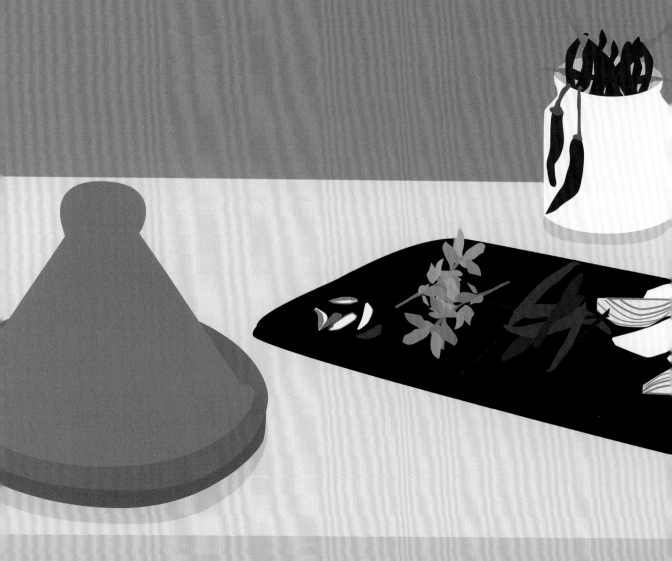

Meat

My dad is a little insane when it comes to cooking. My parents have a big fireplace in their house, and when I was a kid, my dad rigged this metal structure for it that enabled him to cook meat over the fireplace without dripping any fat into it. He would hang whole chickens, racks of lamb, and whole lamb shoulders over it to slow-cook for hours, right there in our living room. While I haven't gone that far in my own home, I think I love working with meat almost as much. It's very technical, which as a chef I appreciate, but also—and maybe this is the hunter in me—there's something celebratory about cooking and eating an animal. You honor its life by treating it with respect, utilizing it properly, and enjoying it with friends and family.

Grilling Guide

One of the first things you see (and definitely the first thing you smell) when you walk into Bavel is the roaring fire taking up almost the entire back wall of the open kitchen. People often think that we cook over that giant flame. But no, the purpose of the fire is to burn down wood into the charcoal we use to light our grill.

There's a level of craveability that you just can't achieve without smoke—the kind of smoke that comes exclusively from grilling with charcoal. It's primal, this ancient drive to cook over fire, and I think our taste buds have evolved to seek out that flavor. Even as chefs around the world come up with new fancy cooking technology like immersion circulators and combi ovens, at the end of the day, we always come back to fire and our love of cooking over real flame.

Is it feasible to burn down your own charcoal from whole logs at home when you're grilling dinner on a weeknight? No. But even a basic Weber charcoal grill will give you an immense amount of flavor that a gas grill just can't provide. It takes a little more time, but the results are worth it.

Grill Setup

With the rack removed, light the coals. After they are ignited, arrange your coals in a slope along the bottom of a charcoal grill, with one side taller and closer to the racks and then gradually sloping to a low pile that's farthest away. These are your temperature zones—high, medium, and low. Then put back the grill rack and allow to preheat for 5 to 10 minutes.

The food at Bavel tends to be less about char than smoke, so most recipes in this book call for keeping the ingredients on medium heat for the majority of the time to absorb as much smoke flavor as possible. If you need to heat up your coals during the cooking process, fan the coals using a sheet pan or a large piece of cardboard.

The Wood

We primarily use almond wood for cooking at Bavel. It provides a delicate smoke and is less frequently cut than oak and cherry, so I feel a little better about using it. Almond wood also burns slightly less hot than other woods; this is important when I'm trying not to roast our line cooks. You can also use almost any other common cooking wood, such as apple, oak, or citrus.

Turmeric Chicken with Toum

When my daughter, Saffron, turned two, we invited a bunch of people to our house for a dinner party. I decided to make this yogurt-marinated chicken, and it was easily the juiciest chicken I'd ever had in my life. The yogurt marinade acts like a brine, tenderizing the meat and making it even juicier than a normal roasted chicken. While the meat cooks, the marinade forms a hard shell around the bird that prevents any juices from escaping, steaming the chicken from the inside out and keeping it super moist. The delicate floral spices of fennel seed, coriander, orange peel, and orange blossom taste incredible on the extra-crispy skin. Serve this alongside rice or with the Salanova Butter Lettuce Salad (page 115), Speckled Lettuce Salad (page 110), or any simple mixed green salad or with Laffa (page 172) and garlic toum.

MAKES 1 CHICKEN; SERVES 2 TO 4

SPECIAL EQUIPMENT:

Kitchen twine (8 inches long)

Instant-read thermometer (optional)

Marinade

1 tablespoon ground turmeric

2 teaspoons ground dried orange peel

1 teaspoon ground fennel seeds

¾ teaspoon ground cumin

1½ teaspoons ground coriander

1 garlic clove, grated with a Microplane

1-inch piece fresh turmeric, peeled and grated with a Microplane

1 tablespoon freshly squeezed orange juice

1 tablespoon plus 1 teaspoon orange blossom water

¾ cup Yogurt (page 81); may substitute store-bought whole milk Greek yogurt

One 3½-pound whole chicken, neck, wing tips, and innards removed

1 tablespoon plus 2½ teaspoons kosher salt

1 teaspoon freshly ground black pepper

Toum (page 197) for serving

To make the marinade: In a bowl, combine the ground turmeric, orange peel, fennel, cumin, coriander, garlic, and fresh turmeric. Then add the orange juice, orange blossom water, and yogurt and stir to combine.

To prepare the chicken: Season the cavity of the chicken with salt and pepper. Rub some of the marinade inside the cavity of the chicken.

Using kitchen twine, tie the legs together. I like to keep the wings loose and not tied so the breasts and wings get crispy.

Evenly season the outside of the chicken with salt and pepper. Place the chicken on a sheet pan and let it sit, uncovered, at room temperature for 30 minutes. Then rub the marinade all over the outside. (It may seem like a lot but use it all.) Transfer the sheet pan, uncovered, to the refrigerator and marinate overnight.

When ready to cook, remove the chicken from the refrigerator and let sit at room temperature for 2 hours prior to cooking. (Cooking the chicken cold will take longer and might dry out the meat.)

CONTINUED

Turmeric Chicken with Toum, continued

Preheat the oven to 450°F. Place the chicken breast-side up on the rack of a roasting pan. Roast for 40 to 50 minutes (if the skin is browning too quickly, decrease the heat to 375°F), until the meat between the leg and thigh feels tender to the touch or using an instant-read thermometer placed in the thigh, the temperature reaches 160° to 165°F. Remove the chicken from the oven and let rest for 15 minutes to let the juices redistribute. Cut off the kitchen twine, carve, and serve with a side of toum.

Toum

MAKES 1 CUP

14 large garlic cloves, roughly
    chopped
2 tablespoons freshly squeezed lemon
    juice
1 heaping teaspoon kosher salt
2 tablespoons orange blossom water
1⅓ cups canola oil

Note: The garlic is what binds the oil with the other liquids to make more of a solidified consistency. If you double this recipe, it will be even easier for your blender to emulsify the ingredients.

Combine the garlic, lemon juice, salt, and orange blossom water in a blender. Pulse on the lowest setting until just combined. Then in a slow and steady stream, add the oil while continuing to blend on low, gradually increasing the speed to medium-high until the mixture has fully emulsified. The consistency should be similar to mayonnaise with some soft peaks.

Store in an airtight container in the refrigerator for up to 1 week. The consistency will thicken slightly after refrigeration.

Aged Duck in Three Parts

You don't find too many duck preparations in traditional Middle Eastern cooking—the terrain has historically been too dry to support much in the way of waterfowl. The flavors of this dish, though, have all the signature warm aromatics of the region: dry mint, cardamom, and orange peel for the kebabs and softer spices like cinnamon, nutmeg, and sumac on the legs.

A roasted whole duck is delicious, but by breaking it down into its parts and cooking them separately, you can really highlight the best characteristics of each. Here, we age the breast meat between 24 and 72 hours to help concentrate the flavor and dry the skin, then we grill the meat over charcoal for a juicy kebab. The legs we simply confit and pan-sear until crisp, and the carcass we use to make a fragrant duck broth similar to a consommé to serve alongside.

While the impact of all three preparations served together is impressive, each part of this dish is super tasty on its own. For that reason, I've broken down the recipe into its elements so you can choose to cook just the kebabs, the legs, or even just get some bones to make a really nice Duck Broth (page 48) for a cold night.

SERVES 4

3 to 4 cups Duck Broth (page 48)

16 cilantro leaves, chiffonade, for garnish

Rendered duck fat for garnish (may substitute olive oil)

Duck Breast Kebabs (page 200)

Pan-Fried Confit Duck Legs (page 201)

Chicory Salad with Calamansi Vinaigrette (page 116); optional

Warm the duck broth and divide it into four small bowls. Garnish each with four leaves of cilantro chiffonade and drizzle with a few drops of rendered duck fat. For each serving, place one kebab next to one leg on a large plate. Serve with the bowls of duck broth and the chicory salad on the side (if using).

CONTINUED

Duck Breast Kebabs

MAKES 4 SKEWERS; SERVES 4

4 duck breasts
4 teaspoons grapeseed oil
4 teaspoons kosher salt
**1 tablespoon plus 1 teaspoon Green
Jerusalem Spice Blend (page 32)**

Note: For this recipe and the Pan-Fried Confit Duck Legs (see opposite), you'll need two whole ducks, separated into breasts, legs, wings, and carcass (ask your butcher to split the carcass into six even pieces for your stock).

Place the duck breasts on a rack-lined sheet pan and refrigerate, uncovered, for 48 to 72 hours to age.

When ready to cook, you will need four skewers. (We use ¾-inch flat metal skewers.) If you are using wooden skewers, soak them in water for at least 1 hour to prevent burning.

Preheat a charcoal grill to have low-, medium-, and high-heat temperature zones (see Grilling Guide on page 192).

Remove the breasts from the refrigerator. Trim off any excess fat, the vein that runs underneath the breast, and any remaining silver skin from each breast. Cut each breast in half lengthwise, then slice each half into four 1-inch pieces. (Each breast will yield eight pieces, enough for one full skewer.)

Puncture each piece of duck with a skewer directly under the fat cap, about 1/16 inch down into the actual breast meat. Using a pastry brush, evenly coat the duck breast pieces with 1 teaspoon of the oil per skewer. Season each skewer with 1 teaspoon of the salt and 1 teaspoon of the spice blend, going a little heavier on the skin side than the meat side.

Place the skewers skin-side down on the grill. Grill over low heat for about 7 to 10 minutes, until the fat has rendered and the skin is golden. Flip the skewers meat-side down, move to medium-high heat and continue to cook for about 2 to 3 minutes, until the meat bounces back slightly when pressed. Remove the skewers from the grill and let rest for 2 minutes before serving.

Pan-Fried Confit Duck Legs

MAKES 4 LEGS; SERVES 4

SPECIAL EQUIPMENT:

Candy or other probe-style thermometer

1 tablespoon kosher salt

½ teaspoon pink curing salt #1

¼ teaspoon freshly ground black pepper

1 tablespoon plus 1½ teaspoons Poultry Spice Blend (page 29)

4 duck legs (see Note, opposite)

2 pounds duck fat

2 teaspoons ground sumac

Pinch of Maldon or other flaky sea salt

In a small bowl, mix together the kosher and pink salts, pepper, and the spice blend. Evenly season each leg on all sides with the spice mixture. Transfer the legs to a sheet pan, cover with plastic wrap, and refrigerate for 4 hours.

Remove the legs from the refrigerator and let sit at room temperature for 1 hour.

Preheat the oven to 225°F. In a 9 by 13-inch baking dish, place the duck legs skin-side up.

In a saucepan fitted with a candy thermometer, melt the duck fat over medium heat until the temperature reaches 225°F. Pour the warmed melted fat over the legs so they are completely submerged. Cover the dish with aluminum foil. Place the baking dish in the oven and bake for 2 hours, then increase the temperature to 250°F and cook for 40 more minutes. Remove the baking dish from the oven, uncover, and let sit for 1 hour at room temperature, then refrigerate, uncovered, until cool. Once completely cooled, cover with plastic wrap and refrigerate overnight. (The legs can be kept in the refrigerator for up to 1 week, stored in the fat.)

When ready to fry, remove the legs from the fat (reserve the fat for frying later) and drain on a rack-lined sheet pan for at least 1 hour.

In an 8-inch cast-iron skillet over high heat, add 3 tablespoons of the leftover duck fat. When the fat begins to sizzle, add two legs skin-side down. Be careful as the confit legs might cause the fat to spit and pop. Fry for 3 minutes, basting the meat side with the fat while it's frying, until golden brown. Then flip skin-side up and continue to fry for about 4 minutes, until golden brown, then transfer to a plate, cover with aluminum foil, and set aside. Repeat the process with the other two legs, then season each leg with ½ teaspoon of the sumac and a couple of flakes of salt.

Lamb Chops

Shepherds and their flocks have roamed the hills of the Middle East for millennia. The same rugged terrain that was difficult to farm provided ample space for raising sheep, and so the cuisines of the region evolved to celebrate lamb and mutton in all its forms. The tender chop is the most prized cut and cooks in just minutes. At Bavel, we quickly grill delicious Te Mana Lamb chops from New Zealand, where the lambs feed on chicory and develop a unique almost-smoky flavor, and then serve them topped with a rustic, herby sauce that's mashed in a mortar and pestle with parsley, garlic, and anchovy. Serve these chops alongside a simple green salad—they don't need anything else.

SERVES 4

2 pounds lamb chops, cold
2½ teaspoons kosher salt
A few turns of freshly ground
    black pepper, to taste
Green Herb Sauce (recipe below)

Preheat a charcoal grill to high heat (see Grilling Guide on page 192). Season the lamb chops with the salt and pepper and place directly onto the grill (the cold meat will prevent overcooking). Grill over high heat for 2½ minutes per side, then transfer to a serving plate and top each chop with about ½ tablespoon of the herb sauce, or more if desired.

Green Herb Sauce

MAKES ¼ CUP

2 garlic cloves
4 oil-packed anchovy fillets, drained
½ teaspoon kosher salt
1 teaspoon granulated sugar
1 cup packed flat-leaf parsley leaves
1 packed cup cilantro leaves
1½ teaspoons freshly squeezed
    lemon juice
1½ teaspoons champagne vinegar
2 tablespoons olive oil
1½ teaspoons Garam Masala (page 35)
¼ teaspoon lemon zest

In a mortar and pestle, smash the garlic, anchovies, salt, and sugar until a paste forms. Add the parsley and cilantro and continue to smash until the herbs have combined with the paste and the color is dark green. Add the lemon juice and vinegar and stir to combine. In a steady stream while stirring, slowly add the oil until emulsified. Finally, gently fold in the garam masala and lemon zest. The sauce can be made up to 24 hours in advance and stored in an airtight container in the refrigerator.

Licorice Lamb Porterhouse

Licorice is not thought of as sweet because the anise flavor tends to dominate, but it is actually 30 to 50 percent sweeter than cane sugar. That's part of the reason it's hard to balance the flavor when cooking with it. Genevieve has a licorice dessert at Bavel, and once was sent the wrong kind of licorice powder by mistake. It sat in the pantry for a month, and finally Genevieve suggested I play with it. At first, I tried it on some lamb chops, which were incredible, but I wanted something different, so instead, I decided to try it on a lamb saddle chop—aka double loin and porterhouse. This chop costs a lot less than a rib chop, but it's also a much tougher cut. Twenty-four hours in a yogurt marinade before grilling helps to break down the proteins, making the meat super tender.

SERVES 4

SPECIAL
EQUIPMENT:

*Instant-read
thermometer
(optional)*

Marinade

1 garlic clove, grated with
  a Microplane

1 teaspoon freshly squeezed
  lime juice

1 cup Yogurt (page 81);
  may substitute store-bought
  whole milk Greek yogurt

1 teaspoon raw licorice powder
  (may substitute 2 teaspoons
  ground fennel seeds)

Four 4- to 6-ounce 1-inch-thick lamb
  porterhouse (may substitute lamb
  chops)

2 tablespoons avocado honey
  (may substitute any honey)

¼ cup plus 1 teaspoon freshly
  squeezed lime juice

½ teaspoon kosher salt, plus more
  for seasoning

½ teaspoon ground dried borage
  flowers (optional)

1 teaspoon rose water

½ cup plus 2 tablespoons olive oil,
  plus more for drizzling

Freshly ground black pepper for
  seasoning

Maldon or other flaky sea salt, to taste

Handful of mustard greens

12 mint leaves

2 sprigs dill, leaves picked

3 bunches chervil, leaves picked

Wedding Rice (page 135)

To make the marinade: In a small bowl, combine the garlic and lime juice and let steep for 3 minutes. Add the yogurt and the licorice powder and mix to combine.

Apply a heaping tablespoon of this marinade on each side of your lamb. Cover and refrigerate for 24 hours.

When ready to cook, remove the lamb from the refrigerator 2 hours before you're ready to grill.

Meanwhile, in a small bowl, whisk together the honey, lime juice, kosher salt, borage flowers (if using), and rose water. Add ½ cup plus 1 tablespoon of the oil in a slow stream while whisking to fully incorporate. Set the vinaigrette aside.

Preheat a charcoal grill or gas grill on high heat (see Grilling Guide on page 192). Season the lamb with a healthy amount of salt and pepper. Lightly coat the lamb with the remaining 1 tablespoon olive oil to avoid sticking. Place the chops on the grill. Sear for 1 minute, rotate 45 degrees, sear for another minute, and then flip. Repeat the searing process on the other side, then remove the lamb from the grill and let rest for at least 4 to 6 minutes. Then return the lamb to the grill until the chops reach your preferred doneness: another 1 to 2 minutes for somewhere between medium-rare and medium, until the meat is firm to the touch; or if you are using an instant-read thermometer until the temperature reaches 135° to 145°F in the center of the loin. Transfer to a plate and drizzle with olive oil and finish with Maldon salt.

In a bowl, combine the mustard greens, mint, dill, and chervil with some of the vinaigrette and salt and pepper to taste. Gently place a handful of the herb salad on top of the plated lamb chop. Serve with the rice.

Lamb Neck Shawarma

One day, chef Musa Dağdeviren and his wife, Zeynap, of the famous Istanbul restaurant Ciya, came to eat at Bavel. They were so nice, and after their meal, they graciously invited me to come visit them in Turkey. Of course, I booked a flight immediately and even arranged for my parents to meet me there as an anniversary present. In the end, only my dad joined me. (There was a mix-up at the airport for my mom, but don't worry, my dad took her for a makeup trip a few months later.) When my dad and I finally got to Istanbul and met up with Musa, one of the first things I told him I wanted to see was how Turkish shawarma was made.

Shawarma is a bit like the hamburger of the Middle East, the ubiquitous comfort food that I couldn't get enough of as a kid. A classic shawarma consists of large pieces of meat—usually turkey, lamb, or beef—that are stacked and roasted on a vertical spit, then shaved into fresh laffa, a traditional Iraqi flatbread, or pita and piled with condiments like tahini, pickles, and salad. Growing up, I used to eat shawarma probably twice a week, especially on Saturdays when my dad, brother, and I would go watch Maccabi Tel Aviv play and grab a shawarma for dinner on the way home.

But it's funny, before that trip to Istanbul, I'd never actually worked in a professional Middle Eastern kitchen before—most of my cooking at Bavel is based on memory and creativity. So, I was thrilled when Musa was generous enough to let me observe in his kitchen at Ciya for two days. During that time, I learned so much about Turkish cooking, especially about what makes Turkish shawarma so great—the marinade, how they stack the meat, how they form kebabs. I'd love to tell you all their secrets, but I'm saving them all for when I open my own shawarma restaurant, something that has always been my dream. If I'm lucky, it may even be open by the time you're reading this.

For now, I cook a different version of shawarma at Bavel, which is not technically shawarma at all. Instead of meat roasted on a spit, I season a whole lamb neck with all of the same warm spices and roast it until it's fall-apart tender and the edges are crisp. We present it whole in the center of the table with a side of Laffa for diners to reach in and pull off hunks by hand. Middle Eastern food is all about eating with your hands—a communal act with big platters of food and with bread as your only utensil, there for grabbing, pinching, scooping, and swiping with your friends and family.

Note: At the restaurant, we butcher our own lambs from Colorado but most high-quality butchers can source lamb necks for you with advance notice. Ask them to remove the neck tendon just above the spine and clean up the bottom.

CONTINUED

SERVES 4 TO 6

1 tablespoon plus 2 teaspoons
 kosher salt

1 teaspoon freshly ground
 black pepper

2 teaspoons Shawarma
 Spice Blend (page 29)

Two 2¼-pound (4½ pounds total)
 lamb necks

5 tablespoons plus 1 teaspoon
 grated yellow onion

4 garlic cloves, grated with
 a Microplane

1 tablespoon grapeseed oil

2 teaspoons freshly squeezed
 lemon juice

Maldon or other flaky sea salt,
 to taste

To Serve

Laffa (page 172)

Assorted pickles (see pages 54 to 60)

Mint Chutney (page 38)

Tahini (page 67)

In a small bowl, mix together the salt, pepper, and spice blend, then evenly and generously coat the lamb necks on all sides.

In another bowl, combine the onion, garlic, and oil. Wearing gloves or using a spatula, evenly coat the seasoned necks in the onion mix. Place on a sheet pan, cover with plastic wrap, and refrigerate overnight.

When ready to cook, remove the pan from the refrigerator and let sit at room temperature for 1 hour.

Preheat the oven to 225°F. Uncover the lamb necks, place the pan in the oven, and roast for 3 hours. Remove from the oven and cover the pan with aluminum foil. Increase the oven temperature to 250°F, return the pan to the oven, and cook for an additional 3 hours. Remove the pan from the oven, uncover, and baste with the fat drippings in the pan. Let sit, uncovered, at room temperature for 30 minutes, basting the lamb every 10 minutes. Then cover each neck with plastic wrap and set aside for another 30 minutes.

Increase the oven temperature to 500°F. Line a sheet pan with a roasting rack. Remove the plastic wrap from the lamb necks and place on the sheet pan. Roast in the oven, uncovered, for 10 minutes. Remove the sheet pan from the oven and season each neck with 1 teaspoon of the lemon juice on top and a pinch of Maldon salt to taste. Serve on top of fresh laffa, along with a side of pickles, chutney, and tahini.

Chapter 7

Family Recipes

These humble specialties that fuse the cooking of my Georgian, Moroccan, Turkish, and Jewish heritage are what nourished my own family as a kid and are the flavors that helped make me who I am today. From the turmeric-stained chicken soup that soothed me when I was sick to the peppery dumplings my brother and I would competitively devour, these are, for me, the tastes of home.

Beef Cheek Tagine

My mother, like me, was born in Morocco in what was then called Mogador (today, it's known as Essaouira), which was located on the Moroccan coast. I was the middle of eleven children, and it seemed like from the day I was born, my mother was always in the kitchen. She would wake up and immediately start cooking, so that every day, the whole family would have a fresh lunch. Then she'd spend the rest of the day working on dinner. She loved going to the souk, the local market, where she would buy vegetables, not by the bunch or the kilo but by the crate, and she never wasted a thing. I remember all the wonderful preserves she'd make with watermelon rinds, lemon peels, and eggplant skins. For the most part, my mother used the same kinds of pots and pans we all use, but on special occasions, she'd cook something in a tagine—the traditional clay cooking vessel used for making slow stews and braises. She'd make a tagine of chicken with vegetables or maybe some fresh Moroccan truffles. And while she never gave me any of her recipes, somehow I've learned to cook many of the things I grew up eating just by instinct, taste, and memory. I'm very proud to be from Morocco.

    —Mirelle Menashe, Ori's mother

SERVES 2 TO 4

2¼ pounds beef cheek, cleaned and cubed into 1¼-inch pieces (may substitute beef short rib)

1 tablespoon plus 1 teaspoon kosher salt

½ teaspoon freshly ground black pepper

2¼ teaspoons granulated sugar

1½ cups apple cider vinegar

2-inch piece fresh ginger, peeled

2 garlic cloves

1 quart Super Stock (page 47); may substitute high-quality store-bought vegetable stock infused with the aromatics from the super stock recipe

7 tablespoons grapeseed oil

2 tablespoons unsalted butter

3 cups diced yellow onion

1 fresh bay leaf or 1 dry bay leaf

3 tablespoons Ras el Hanout (page 27)

1 tablespoon brown sugar

1 serrano chile, sliced

1 prune, quartered

4 dried apricots, quartered

Cilantro leaves and stems for garnish

Rice, couscous, or mashed potatoes for serving

Season the beef cheek with the salt, black pepper, and granulated sugar. Let rest for 10 minutes.

In a blender, puree the vinegar, ginger, and garlic. Place the seasoned beef cheeks in a bowl, pour the liquid over the meat, and mix to coat. Cover with plastic wrap and let marinate in the refrigerator overnight or for up to 24 hours.

Remove the beef cheeks from the refrigerator. Drain, reserving the liquid, and bring to room temperature. Transfer the reserved marinade to a small saucepan and cook over low heat until reduced by half. Set aside.

In a separate small saucepan, bring the stock to a boil. Preheat the oven to 325°F.

Add 1 tablespoon of the oil and ½ tablespoon of the butter to a sauté pan and place over high heat. Add one-quarter of the meat and sear on both sides until golden, about 4 minutes, then transfer to a plate with a slotted spoon and set aside. Repeat this process, adding another 1 tablespoon of the oil and ½ tablespoon of the butter to the pan before adding another one-quarter of the meat, until all the meat has been seared.

CONTINUED

Beef Cheek Tagine, continued

Wipe the pan clean, then return to the stove over high heat and add the remaining 3 tablespoons oil. Add the onion and bay leaf and cook for 4 to 5 minutes, until the onion is translucent, stirring to avoid browning. Remove the pan from the heat and add the ras el hanout. Stir to coat the onions and bloom the spices for about 1 minute. Add the brown sugar and the reduced marinade liquid and stir to combine. Transfer the onion mixture to a 6-quart baking dish and top with the seared beef cheeks. Pour the hot stock over the beef cheeks. Then cover the dish with aluminum foil. Bake for 2½ hours, until the meat is fork-tender and has fully broken down. Remove the cheeks from the oven and uncover. Add the sliced serrano chile and let rest, uncovered, for 1 hour. The cheeks can be prepared up to 1 day ahead and stored, covered, in the refrigerator overnight. To reheat, preheat the oven to 325°F. Remove the beef cheeks from the refrigerator and skim the fat off the top. Cook for about 30 minutes, until the dish reaches your desired temperature.

To serve, transfer the cheeks to a large serving bowl or tagine and top with the prune and apricots. Garnish with cilantro leaves. Serve with a side of rice, couscous, or mashed potatoes.

Hingali (Dumplings)

There was always good food in my house as a child. My mother was from Georgia, and she was an incredible cook. She'd make dishes from my father's homeland on the border of Iran and Turkey, like Persian rice with spiced vegetables. She could outcook the neighbors with traditional Jewish foods—nobody in Israel made a better gefilte fish than my mother. But her specialty was traditional foods from her home country, like rich Georgian stews and hundreds of peppery, beef-filled hingali dumplings. When I was a child, I remember my mother and my aunt sitting in the kitchen from early in the morning making five to six hundred hingali dumplings at a time by hand. The entire family would then come over to the house and eat them, and my brother and I would compete to see who could eat the most. Today, as cooking has become one of my greatest passions, Ori and his brother are now competing to eat as many of *my* hingali as they can.

—Gideon Menashe, Ori's father

Note: These are great to make in giant batches and freeze to use throughout the week. My grandmother always served hers in a light broth of just salted garlic-infused water. I like to take a small nibble of a dumpling, spoon a little of the garlic water inside, and eat it whole. Also, when forming the dumplings, it's important to keep the meat mixture cold so the fat doesn't melt when you're handling it.

MAKES ABOUT 60 DUMPLINGS; SERVES 4 TO 6

SPECIAL EQUIPMENT:

Pasta sheeter

3-inch round biscuit or cookie cutter

Filling

1 cup grapeseed oil

2 large yellow onions, diced small

3 tablespoons kosher salt

2 tablespoons freshly ground black pepper

2¼ pounds ground chuck, 75% lean/ 25% fat (may substitute 80%/20%)

Dough

7⅓ cups all-purpose flour, plus more for dusting

1¾ cups water

3 eggs

1 tablespoon plus 1 teaspoon kosher salt

1 quart boiling water

2 large garlic cloves, grated with a Microplane

6 tablespoons kosher salt

2 quarts room temperature water

To make the filling: In a large saucepan over high heat, add the oil and onion and cook until the onion is translucent, 6 to 7 minutes. Then add the salt, pepper, and beef and cook for 10 to 12 minutes more, breaking up the beef with a wooden spoon or spatula as it cooks. Once the meat is browned, transfer the mixture to a bowl and let cool. Then cover with plastic wrap and refrigerate overnight.

To make the dough: Place the flour, water, eggs, and salt in the bowl of a stand mixer fitted with the dough hook attachment. Combine on the lowest speed for 10 minutes, until the mixture pulls from the sides of the bowl and has become one complete dough mass. (If your mixer can't handle the density of the dough, slowly add a little more water.) Turn the dough out onto the counter and gently knead into a round ball. Wrap the dough ball in plastic wrap and refrigerate for at least 3 hours or up to 3 days.

CONTINUED

Hingali (Dumplings), continued

We use an Imperia pasta sheeter, turning the dial settings as follows: 10, 8, 6, 4, 3.

Remove the dough from the refrigerator and divide into four equal pieces. While you're working with one piece, keep the others wrapped in plastic to prevent them from drying out. Lightly dust the piece of dough with flour and flatten slightly with your hands. Pass the piece of flattened dough through a pasta sheeter* one time on the widest setting. Fold the dough in half to create more of a rectangle, then pass the dough through the widest setting one more time, always leading with the thickest end of the dough. Repeat the process, decreasing the thickness setting by one notch each time, until you have a long rectangle of dough about 1/16 inch thick, about three to four more times. If at any point the dough gets sticky, lightly flour each side. Alternatively, roll out the dough on a smooth, lightly floured surface with a rolling pin until 1/16 inch thick.

Using a 3-inch round biscuit cutter, punch out circles of the dough by lining up the cutter where you want to cut, then press down and twist. Reserve the scraps of dough to add into the next quarter of dough. Line up the circles on a lightly floured surface or sheet pan for filling.

Line a sheet pan with a dry kitchen towel. Remove the meat mixture from the refrigerator and while it's still cold, add ¾ tablespoon of the filling in the center of each dough circle. Fold the circle in half over the filling to form a half-moon, pressing the outside edge with your fingers to seal the meat inside. If your dumplings aren't sealing, dip a finger in water and wet the edge of the dumpling to create a better seal. Transfer the finished dumplings to the prepared sheet pan and cover with another dry kitchen towel. Let rest for 1 to 2 hours at room temperature.

Repeat the whole process with all the remaining dough and filling, resting each batch for 1 to 2 hours total. You can freeze the uncooked dumplings at this point for up to 3 weeks and cook, frozen, when ready. Any leftover meat mixture can be stored in an airtight container in the refrigerator, then later heated up and served over Wedding Rice, without the flower garnish (page 135).

When ready to cook, combine the boiling water, garlic, and 2 tablespoons of the salt in a large serving bowl and set aside.

In a large pot, bring the 2 quarts water and the remaining 4 tablespoons salt to a boil. Once boiling, gently place twenty dumplings into the boiling water and cook for 4 minutes. Using a slotted spoon or spider, gently transfer the dumplings from the boiling water to the bowl of garlic water. Repeat the process until all of the dumplings have been cooked. To serve, ladle an equal number of dumplings and a bit of garlic water into individual bowls. Serve immediately.

Grandmother's Meatballs (Chefte)

My paternal grandmother was the kind of person whom you couldn't help but notice the minute she walked into a room. She was a strong personality but also fiercely maternal and one of my first role models as a cook. I remember she would often show up at our house lugging two giant pots—one filled with okra and rice and the other with some kind of delicious braise. On Fridays, we would go to her place for Shabbat, and while the grown-ups were busy talking and pouring wine, she would be in the kitchen cooking feasts and sneaking bits of candy into all the kids' pockets.

My grandmother was born in Georgia, raised in Turkey, and settled in Israel, and the food she cooked was a mix of those flavors and influences. The delicate seasoning of these poached bulgur-and-beef meatballs closely reflects her varied roots, as does the turmeric-spiked chicken broth in which she poached them. As kids, we would have these warm with boiled potatoes for dinner, and the next day we'd eat them chilled, almost like cold cuts, wrapped in watercress and dipped in tahini. I still savor those cold leftover snacks when I make a batch of meatballs for my own family today.

MAKES 9 MEATBALLS; SERVES 3 TO 4

1½ cups coarse ground cracked bulgur wheat

1 cup room temperature water

1¼ pounds ground beef, 75% lean/ 25% fat (may substitute 80%/20%)

1 yellow onion, diced

3 tablespoons plus 2 teaspoons kosher salt

½ teaspoon freshly ground black pepper

1 tablespoon ground cumin

1 tablespoon Marash pepper (may substitute ground chile flakes)

2 quarts Turmeric-Chicken Stock (page 49)

2 russet or Yukon gold potatoes, peeled and cut into ¾-inch dice

Watercress for serving (optional)

Tahini (page 67) for serving (optional)

In a medium bowl, add the bulgur and pour the water over to cover. Let sit until the bulgur has absorbed all the water, about 10 minutes. Add the bulgur to the bowl of a food processor along with the beef, onion, 2 tablespoons plus 1 teaspoon of the salt, black pepper, cumin, and Marash pepper. Blend the mixture for 2 to 3 minutes, until emulsified and pasty. Transfer to a bowl, cover with plastic wrap, and refrigerate overnight.

Remove the bowl from the refrigerator. Wet your hands and form the cold meat into nine ½-cup oblong meatballs.

In a large saucepan over high heat, bring the stock and the remaining 1 tablespoon plus 1 teaspoon salt to a boil. Using a slotted spoon, gently place each meatball into the stock. Make sure the meatballs don't touch one another or they will stick. Once all of the meatballs have been added to the pot, the stock volume should have risen to cover the meatballs. Return the stock to a boil, then decrease the heat to a simmer and cook, uncovered, for 20 minutes. And the potatoes and simmer for another 10 minutes, until the potatoes are soft and the meatballs are cooked through. Remove from the heat and let cool for 15 minutes.

Ladle the broth, meatballs, and potatoes into four bowls. Serve with a side of watercress and tahini (if desired).

Peshalo (Noodle Soup)

Most families have their own version of the cure-all soup for when someone's sick, and this was ours. I had a ton of ear infections as a child, and whenever I was sick, my grandmother would bring over a huge pot of peshalo, which was loaded with cabbage, garbanzo beans, thick handmade noodles she had sliced with a pizza cutter, and a bright yellow broth spiked with her secret ingredient: chicken-flavored bouillon cubes. This version of the soup is equally bright, but here the deep flavor doesn't come from any MSG-laden cubes but rather from chicken bones, and it's full of ingredients like spinach, cabbage, and carrots—healthy stuff that's very healing.

SERVES 4

1 cup dried garbanzo beans

6 cups water, plus more for soaking

1 teaspoon baking soda

2 quarts Turmeric-Chicken Stock (page 49)

2 tablespoons kosher salt

1 pound savoy cabbage, cut into 1-inch dice

2 medium carrots, peeled and diced into ½-inch cubes

1 pound spinach

Soup Noodles (page 225)

1 teaspoon ground turmeric

1 teaspoon freshly ground black pepper

Place the beans in a large bowl or other container, cover with water, and let soak overnight. Drain the beans and rinse thoroughly.

Preheat the oven to 325°F. In a large bowl, add the beans and baking soda and toss to coat. Evenly spread the beans on a sheet pan and bake for 8 minutes.

In a large pot over high heat, add the water and the baked beans. Bring the water to a boil, then decrease the heat to a simmer. Simmer uncovered, skimming off any foam that builds up on the surface with a spoon, for about 30 minutes, until the beans are tender but not falling apart. Remove from the heat and let the beans rest in the liquid for 5 minutes.

In a large stockpot over high heat, add the stock and salt and bring to a boil, then decrease the heat to a simmer. Drain the cooked garbanzo beans and add them to the pot along with the cabbage and carrots and cook for 10 minutes. Add the spinach and let wilt for 1 to 2 minutes, then add the noodles, turmeric, and pepper. Cook for 3 to 5 minutes, until the noodles are cooked through. Serve immediately in individual bowls.

CONTINUED

Soup Noodles

MAKES 14 OUNCES

SPECIAL
EQUIPMENT:

Pasta sheeter

1½ cups plus ⅓ cup all-purpose flour,
   plus more for dusting
¼ cup plus 2 tablespoons water
1 egg
1 egg yolk
1 teaspoon kosher salt

*We use an Imperia pasta sheeter, turning the dial settings
as follows: 10, 8, 6, 4, 3.*

Place the flour, water, egg, egg yolk, and salt in the bowl of a stand mixer fitted with the dough hook attachment. Mix on the lowest speed for 4 to 6 minutes, until the dough forms a single mass that begins to pull away from the sides of the bowl. (If your mixer can't handle the density of the dough, slowly add a little more water to increase the hydration.)

Turn the dough out onto a counter dusted with flour and knead by hand, rotating the dough 90 degrees with each knead, for an additional 4 to 6 minutes, for a total of 10 minutes. Form the dough into a ball and wrap in plastic wrap or store in an airtight plastic bag. Refrigerate for at least 3 hours or up to 3 days.

Remove the dough from the refrigerator and cut into four equal pieces. Wrap up the other three pieces to keep them from drying out while working. Lightly flour the dough and flatten a little with your fingers. Using a pasta sheeter,* pass the dough quarter through the sheeter one time on the widest setting. Fold the edges of the dough inward to form a rectangle, then flip the dough over and pass through the sheeter on the widest setting one more time. Keep passing the dough through the sheeter, progressively narrowing the settings, until you have a long, very thin strip of dough about 1⁄16 inch thick. If at any point the dough gets sticky, lightly flour each side. Alternatively, roll out the dough on a smooth, lightly floured surface with a rolling pin until 1⁄16 inch thick.

Lay the sheet of dough out on a floured flat surface. Using a pizza cutter or sharp knife, cut the dough into ½-inch-wide strips. The shape should be rustic, so they don't need to be perfectly even. Repeat the entire process with the remaining three portions of dough. The noodles can be rolled and cut up to 2 days in advance. Lightly coat them with flour and store in small, loosely packed bundles inside of an airtight container in the refrigerator.

Chapter 8

Drinks

I was only given one real piece of direction when I started as the bar manager for Bavel: no Middle Eastern spices in the cocktails. It wasn't a hard rule, but because our aim was to make every drink as food friendly as possible, too many spices in a cocktail would amplify those flavors in the food and throw both the dish and the drink out of balance. From there, I explored the flavors and fragrances of the Middle East, learning as much as I could about new ingredients like sumac and hedysarum or black lime and date molasses. I also looked to the space for inspiration, trying to capture its light and airy vibe with equally bright and slightly more floral versions of classic cocktails. The signature drink at Bestia is an old fashioned, washed with pork fat, so we continued that idea here at Bavel with a lamb fat–washed bourbon cocktail, using the kitchen's butchery scraps. The result, I hope, is a list of original delicious drinks that complement the whole of Bavel in flavor and spirit.

—Ricky Yarnall, Bavel bar director

Zivah

I always try to make sure that my cocktail menu has a good balance. The Zivah was my choice for Bavel's "vodka cocktail," offering an approachable flavor profile using somewhat more challenging ingredients. I wanted to push beyond the usual expectations of a vodka drink, and I came up with a riff on a gimlet that substitutes vodka and aquavit for the normal botanicals found in gin. House-made celery syrup shows a bitter complexity and enough sweetness to temper out the acidic lime juice, creating a beautiful balance of savory herbs next to the sweet and the sour. We shake the drink with an egg white, which results in a creamy and silky mouthfeel. Finally, we top off the drink with edible marigold flowers, so you get this floral note on the nose with the first sip.

MAKES 1 DRINK

1 ounce medium-bodied vodka*
1 ounce aquavit**
1 ounce freshly squeezed lime juice
¾ ounce Celery Syrup (recipe below)
Pinch of salt
1 egg white
Dried marigold flowers or chamomile
    blossoms for garnish (optional)

Shake everything in a cocktail shaker without ice until frothy. Add ice to the cocktail shaker and shake again very hard. Strain through a fine-mesh strainer into a chilled cocktail glass. Garnish with dried marigold flowers.

*We use St. George vodka.

**We use Blinking Owl aquavit.

Celery Syrup

MAKES ABOUT 2 CUPS

1 cup raw celery juice
    (may substitute store-bought
    cold-pressed celery juice)
1¾ cups granulated sugar

Combine the celery juice and sugar and whisk to dissolve the sugar (this might take several minutes). Store in an airtight container in the refrigerator for up to 3 days.

Nissim

This drink was a collaboration—one of the first drinks offered up for the menu by one of our opening bartenders, Aly Iwamoto. The drink started as a sort of stirred Negroni, but to fit into the light, bright, floral playbook of Bavel, we decided to lengthen it a bit with pineapple juice and a splash of soda water, adding some honey for sweetness and body. The result is a bittersweet and refreshing grassy cooler that's become a menu staple.

MAKES 1 DRINK

1 ounce Singani brandy* (may substitute Pisco brandy)

½ ounce Cocchi Americano**

¼ ounce Dolin Genepy†

¼ ounce Suze

½ ounce fresh pineapple juice (may substitute canned or bottled juice)

¾ ounce Honey Syrup (recipe below)

¾ ounce freshly squeezed lemon juice

Soda water for topping off

1 sprig dill for garnish

In a cocktail shaker, combine the brandy, Cocchi Americano, Dolin Genepy, Suze, pineapple juice, syrup, and lemon juice with 1 or 2 pieces of ice and shake until the ice melts. Pour over ice into a collins glass. Top off with soda water and garnish with the dill.

*Singani brandy is a Bolivian grape brandy with a high-tone floral character. Try it in a daiquiri.

**Cocchi Americano is an aperitivo spirit with a slightly bitter-orange flavor profile. Try it in a spritz!

†Dolin Genepy is an alpine-style liqueur. Try a splash in your whiskey sour. Can substitute green chartreuse if you are in dire straits.

Honey Syrup

MAKES 1 TO 1¼ CUPS

1 cup honey

⅓ cup water

Combine the honey and water in a small container and stir until thoroughly combined. Store in an airtight container in the refrigerator for up to 2 weeks.

Dalia

The Dalia is based on a classic cocktail called the Poet's Dream, which is like a gin martini with a little bit of Bénédictine in it. In the traditional version, I love the way the warming herbs of the Bénédictine play with the cooling flavors of the dry vermouth and gin. In our version, we're still playing with those warming and cooling flavors, but we push it a little further in either direction. Tarragon in the gin cools it off even further, while the crème de cacao plays that warming role. The drink is a very delicate nod to those bittersweet chocolate oranges you used to crack open as a kid. You don't really taste the chocolate too much, but you can feel it in that little bit of extra body to what's really just a classic gin martini through and through.

MAKES 1 DRINK

2 ounces Tarragon-Infused Gin
  (recipe below)
¾ ounce dry vermouth
¼ ounce high-quality crème de cacao*
2 dashes orange bitters
Orange peel strip for garnish

Stir all the ingredients in a mixing glass with ice. Strain into a chilled cocktail glass and garnish with the orange peel.

We use Tempus Fugit crème de cacao.

Tarragon-Infused Gin

MAKES 1 LITER

¼ cup packed tarragon leaves
1 liter dry gin*

In a large bowl or other container, steep the leaves in the dry gin for 30 to 45 minutes. Using a sieve, strain out the leaves and funnel the gin back into the original bottle or store in another airtight container. It will keep in the refrigerator for up to 2 weeks.

We use Fords gin.

Chapter 9

Desserts

The way we like to see it, dessert doesn't have to mean "sugary." A great dessert can be palate cleansing, like a pomegranate-hibiscus sorbet, or refreshing, like a coconut tapioca pudding. It can even be a little bitter, like some barely sweet chocolate donuts, or purely comforting, like a moist slice of apple-prune cake. There are so many different ways to round out a meal—so much room for play and experimentation around the concept of dessert. In other words, "sweet" is just the start.

When I was designing the pastry menu at our first restaurant, Bestia, I looked to the nostalgic treats of my childhood, the flavors of retro Americana like strawberry shortcake bars and apple cider donuts. Bavel, though, was different. While growing up with an Egyptian father provided a jumping-off point to draw from—candy dishes full of rose water nougat and platters of dates set out for company—I decided to look further afield, to the spices and aromas of the whole Middle East.

Clove, cardamom, licorice, allspice—these are all common flavors in Middle Eastern cooking, but you'll most often experience them in savory dishes. Traditional Middle Eastern desserts tend to skew sugary and floral, with a lot of orange blossom water, rose water, honey, and dates. I love all those flavors, but I wanted to add some darker, more savory notes as well, so I took many of the fragrances found in the region's savory dishes and incorporated them into pastry.

From there, it was just about finding the best vehicle to suit each flavor. Clove, for instance, can be almost numbing on your tongue if used too aggressively. But when mixed with sugar and tossed with still-warm donuts, you get just the fragrance of clove on your nose when you bite into it, without it overwhelming your palate. Licorice, too, is ten times as sweet as sugar and can easily become cloying. But the fat and dairy of a super-rich ice cream balances that licorice flavor, making it more caramelly than harsh.

While you won't find our signature licorice bonbon recipe in this book (sourcing the right licorice powder is downright impossible), I do include some of my favorite home recipes that reflect my life outside of work, like the Spiced Camp Cake (page 272) I bake for family gatherings and the Earl Grey Chai Blend (page 283) I make for my staff. In every case, my hope is that the recipes here empower you to experiment with new flavors and techniques in your baking. Because as I said, dessert is about so much more than sweet.

—**Genevieve**

Measuring

I only feature weight measurements for certain recipes where I think even subtle inaccuracies will affect the final product. So if you see a weight in these recipes, I recommend using it. As we've said before, weighing is actually easier than measuring. With weighing, you can gather your ingredients, weigh them out, assemble your recipe, and have a cake in the oven in just a few minutes—and most of the time, you will be using just one or two bowls in the process. It takes me close to twice as long to use cups and measuring spoons.

The Quality of Ingredients

When you're trying to extract flavors from raw ingredients, make sure those ingredients are the highest quality possible. Buy fruit at its peak season and look for organic whenever possible. For dried fruit like dates and prunes, choose ones that are still soft, not hard-as-a-rock, and naturally dried. (Make sure there's no sulfur dioxide listed in the ingredients of your dried fruit, as not only does it slightly alter the taste but it's also probably not good for you.)

Butter

Butter in all dessert recipes is unsalted unless otherwise noted.

To brown butter: Melt butter in a saucepan over high heat. Once the butter has melted, turn the heat to low and let cook until the solids settle to the bottom of the pan and the butter turns a dark brown. Let cool, then transfer to an airtight container and refrigerate for up to 1 month.

Apple-Prune Cake

Ori and I both love a classic sticky toffee pudding, but it can be aggressively sweet. All of that sugar serves a purpose, though, providing moisture for the cake's signature puddinglike texture. If you cut back on the sugar and dates, the cake dries out and loses flavor; add in more fat and it becomes too heavy. My solution, then, is to use apples and prunes, both of which add moisture and that great sharp, sticky flavor but without the cloying sweetness. Instead of putting the dates in the cake, I work them into a buttery sauce that completes the elegant dessert. Or leave the cake plain and enjoy a slice for breakfast or afternoon tea.

SERVES 8

1 cup (125g) lightly packed chopped prunes

2 tablespoons (30g) Armagnac; if omitting alcohol, substitute an additional 2 tablespoons (30g) apple cider

1 cup (240g) apple cider

1⅓ cups (155g) all-purpose flour

⅓ cup (38g) einkorn flour (may substitute whole-wheat pastry flour)

2¼ teaspoons baking powder

1 teaspoon baking soda

½ teaspoon kosher salt

2½ teaspoons ground cardamom

1 teaspoon ground cinnamon

1 cup (120g) firmly packed grated Pink Lady apples (may substitute any other crisp, tart apple)

7 tablespoons (100g) butter, plus more for greasing

½ cup (90g) lightly packed muscovado sugar (may substitute light brown sugar)

½ teaspoon vanilla extract

2 eggs

Toffee Sauce (page 243); or use your own favorite toffee sauce recipe

Whipped Crème Fraîche (page 243)

In a bowl, combine the prunes, Armagnac, and apple cider. Cover and let soak for at least 1 hour or up to overnight in the refrigerator.

In a separate bowl, combine the all-purpose and einkorn flours, baking powder, baking soda, salt, cardamom, and cinnamon and thoroughly whisk together. Set aside.

After at least 1 hour of soaking, add the prune mixture to a saucepan over medium-low heat and cook until the prunes are soft and mostly broken down, 5 to 7 minutes. Set aside and let cool to room temperature, then stir in the apples.

Preheat the oven to 350°F. Generously butter a 9-inch cake pan.

In a stand mixer fitted with the paddle attachment, cream the butter and sugar on medium speed until light and fluffy, 7 to 10 minutes. Scrape down the bowl, then add the vanilla and cream until combined. Scrape down the bowl once again and add the eggs, one at a time, scraping down the bowl after each addition. Once the eggs are fully incorporated, on the lowest speed, alternate adding the wet and dry ingredients in two batches each, starting with the wet and ending with the dry and scraping down the bowl after each addition. Be sure not to overmix.

Pour the batter into the pan and bake for about 24 minutes, until golden brown and a toothpick inserted into the middle comes out with moist crumbs and no wet batter. Let the cake cool in the pan for 15 to 20 minutes, then slice and serve while still warm, with warm toffee sauce and a dollop of whipped crème fraîche on the side. If not serving right away,

CONTINUED

leave the cake in the pan to cool completely. When ready to serve, rewarm the cake in the pan in the oven at 350°F for 5 to 7 minutes, until warm. Then slice and serve. If you wish to present the cake whole, cool it in the pan for 15 to 20 minutes, then turn the full cake out of the pan onto a serving platter.

Toffee Sauce

MAKES 1 CUP

7 tablespoons (150g) date syrup*
¼ cup (45g) lightly packed muscovado sugar (may substitute light brown sugar)
½ teaspoon kosher salt
10 tablespoons (140g) butter
½ cup (120g) heavy whipping cream

Combine the date syrup, sugar, salt, butter, and cream in a small saucepan and place over medium heat. Whisk to thoroughly combine. Remove from the heat once the sauce comes together. Use immediately or store in an airtight container in the refrigerator for up to 3 days. Reheat in a saucepan, while stirring with a spoon or whisk, until hot.

You can find date syrup in most Middle Eastern markets.

Whipped Crème Fraîche

MAKES 1 CUP

½ cup (120g) heavy whipping cream
½ cup (120g) crème fraîche

In a small bowl, combine the cream and crème fraîche. Whisk vigorously until firm peaks form. Serve immediately.

Strawberry-Sumac Pastry with Pistachio Ice Cream

Strawberries love sour. That's why you'll so often find them paired with sour ingredients like lemon and rhubarb. Sumac has an earthy, woodsy, almost cranberry-like sourness that complements the strawberries perfectly. I wanted to incorporate that flavor combination into a traditional Middle Eastern–style cheese pastry, but in a way that's more fresh than heavy and sweet. The result is this: a flaky pastry dough that we form into a delicate hand pie filled with candied strawberries, sumac, and a bit of salty cheese to balance the concentrated sweetness of the berries. We serve it with some Yogurt Whipped Cream and Pistachio Ice Cream, but both the pastry and the ice cream are delicious on their own.

MAKES 9 INDIVIDUAL PASTRIES

Pastry Dough

2⅓ cups (270g) all-purpose flour, plus more for dusting

¾ teaspoon (3g) kosher salt

4 teaspoons (18g) granulated sugar, plus more for coating

¾ cup (170g) butter, cubed, plus more at room temperature for brushing the tops

¼ to ½ cup (60 to 120g) ice-cold water

1 egg

1 cup plus 2 tablespoons Ricotta-Yogurt Filling (page 246)

1 cup Strawberry-Sumac Filling (page 247)

2¼ cups Pistachio Ice Cream (page 248); optional

Yogurt Whipped Cream (page 248)

To make the pastry dough: In the bowl of a stand mixer fitted with the whisk attachment, add the flour, salt, and sugar and whisk to combine. Once the butter cubes are pliable but not too soft, add them to the flour mixture and toss to coat the butter. Then, with your hands, pick up each butter cube and smash it between your palms into a thin, flat disk about ⅛ inch thick and drop it back into the bowl. Repeat the process, until all of the cubes have been flattened. Then, using your fingers, gently shred the butter disks until the flour-coated disks are shaggy.

Put the bowl onto the stand mixer fitted with the paddle attachment. With the mixer on the lowest speed, drizzle in ¼ cup (60g) of the water and mix until just incorporated. Stop the mixer and finish mixing gently by hand. If the dough feels too dry, add up to an additional ¼ cup (60g) water. The finished dough should feel hydrated, and if you squeeze a small handful, it should hold together without being mushy. Knead the dough gently in the bowl until it fully incorporates; do not overmix, as you don't want to break up the butter too much.

Divide the dough into two balls, one ball slightly larger (60g heavier) than the other. Wrap each dough ball in plastic wrap and then flatten each into a 1-inch-thick disk. The dough should be well marbled with butter. If there are any large chunks, break them up with your fingers. Refrigerate for at least 2 hours or up to 24 hours before rolling.

Pull the dough out of the refrigerator, and on a lightly floured work surface, roll out the larger portion ⅛ inch thick. Cut into 4½-inch squares (squares are

CONTINUED

the easiest way to cut pastry dough, but you can cut these in any shape you desire). Then cut four venting slits on a diagonal, pointing towards the center of the pastry, in the corners of these larger pastry squares. Brush the tops with butter and lightly coat with sugar.

Roll out the smaller portion of dough on a lightly floured work surface ⅛ inch thick. Cut into 4-inch squares.

Beat the egg in a small bowl. Using a pastry brush or your finger, paint a ¼-inch border of egg wash around the edge of the smaller square.

Preheat the oven to 375°F. Line a baking sheet with parchment paper.

Lay out the smaller dough squares evenly on the prepared baking sheet. To each, add 2 tablespoons of the yogurt filling and top with 1½ tablespoons of the strawberry filling. Place a buttered and sugared larger square on top of the filling. Gently press the edges with your fingers to seal. Bake for 23 minutes, until the tops are light golden brown.

The pastries can be made 1 day in advance. To reheat, warm the pastries in a 350°F oven for 3 to 4 minutes. Serve on a plate with a dollop of yogurt whipped cream and a scoop of pistachio ice cream (if using).

Ricotta-Yogurt Filling

MAKES ABOUT 2 CUPS

1 cup (227g) whole milk ricotta
  or sheep's milk ricotta
1 cup (227g) Yogurt (page 81)
  (may substitute store-bought
  whole milk Greek yogurt)
1 egg
½ cup (100g) granulated sugar
¼ teaspoon kosher salt
1 tablespoon freshly squeezed
  lemon juice

In a small bowl, combine the ricotta, yogurt, egg, sugar, salt, and lemon juice and whisk until smooth.

Note: Add leftover filling into a ramekin and bake at 350°F for 15 to 20 minutes, or until puffed and lightly golden. Spread over toast with a drizzle of honey and Maldon salt. Yum.

Strawberry-Sumac Filling

MAKES 2 CUPS

About 6½ cups (2 pounds / 900g)
fresh strawberries

1¼ cups (250g) granulated sugar

½ teaspoon (3g) citric acid

1½ teaspoons (7g) fraise des bois
liqueur (optional; if omitting,
add 1½ teaspoons more of the
strawberry liquid)

1½ teaspoons (3g) ground sumac

Note: This is a 4-day process, and the final filling can
be stored in an airtight container in the refrigerator for
up to 1 month. Any leftover filling can be used over
yogurt, granola, or as a topping for waffles or pancakes
in the morning. Don't throw out any extra strawberry
liquid: it can be used to make an amazing strawberry
lemonade, or poured over ice and mixed with soda
water for a delicious strawberry soda.

Wash, stem, and quarter the strawberries. In a large
container or bowl, add the strawberries and sugar.
Stir to combine, cover, and let sit at room temperature for 24 hours to macerate. Drain the strawberries
into a colander or chinois set over a medium saucepan. Transfer the drained strawberries to a bowl and
set aside.

Place the saucepan with the strawberry liquid over
high heat and bring to a boil. Pour the boiling liquid
over the strawberries in the bowl. Let sit, uncovered,
until the strawberries cool to room temperature. Cover
and store in the refrigerator overnight. Over the next
3 days, repeat the draining, boiling, and steeping process once more each day.

After the third boil, add the strawberries and their
liquid to a medium saucepan over low heat and gently
bring to a simmer. Once a simmer is reached, remove
from the heat and let cool to room temperature.
Transfer to a bowl, cover, and refrigerate overnight.

The next day, drain the strawberries, reserving
⅓ cup (90g) liquid (see Note). In a medium saucepan
over high heat, add the cooked strawberries, reserved
liquid, citric acid, liqueur, and sumac. Bring to a boil.
Remove from the heat and let cool to room temperature. The filling is ready to use once it has cooled.

CONTINUED

Pistachio Ice Cream

MAKES ABOUT 5 CUPS

SPECIAL
EQUIPMENT:

*Immersion
blender*

*Ice cream
maker*

2 cups (480g) heavy whipping cream
2 cups (460g) whole milk
Pinch of kosher salt
1¼ cups (250g) granulated sugar
9 egg yolks
1⅓ cups (170g) raw pistachios
½ teaspoon almond extract
Pinch of citric acid
1 tablespoon plus 1 teaspoon
   amaretto
1 tablespoon pistachio oil

In a large saucepan over high heat, add the cream, 1 cup (230g) of the milk, salt, and 1 cup (200g) of the sugar. Cook until very hot and steaming, about 5 minutes. Remove from the heat.

In a medium bowl, add the egg yolks and the remaining ¼ cup (50g) sugar and whisk to combine. Temper the yolks by adding half of the cream mixture to the egg-sugar mixture while whisking to combine, then slowly add the remaining cream mixture while whisking. Add the tempered egg-cream mixture back to the saucepan and cook over low heat, stirring con-tinuously with a spatula, until it's thick enough to coat the back of a spoon, about 10 minutes. Strain the mix-ture through a fine-mesh sieve or chinois into a large bowl. Add the remaining 1 cup (230g) milk and stir to combine. Transfer the mixture to a medium bowl and cover the bowl with plastic wrap, pressing it onto the surface of the ice cream base to avoid forming a skin, and refrigerate until very cold, 8 hours or overnight.

Grind the pistachios in either a food processor or spice grinder until they are as fine as you can get them. Set aside in an airtight container until your base is chilled and ready to churn.

Add the ground pistachios, almond extract, citric acid, amaretto, and pistachio oil to the chilled ice cream base. Puree the mixture with an immersion blender or blender until smooth, 1 to 2 minutes.

Transfer the mixture to an ice cream machine and churn according to the manufacturer's instructions. Store in an airtight container in the freezer for up to 1 week.

Yogurt Whipped Cream

MAKES 1 CUP

½ cup (113g) Yogurt (page 81)
   (may substitute store-bought
   whole milk Greek yogurt)
½ cup (120g) heavy whipping cream
1 tablespoon (13g) granulated sugar

In a small bowl, add the yogurt, cream, and sugar and stir to combine. Whip with a whisk or a hand mixer until soft peaks form. Chill in an airtight container in the refrigerator until ready to use or no longer than 3 hours.

Rose-Clove Donuts with Sherry Diplomat Cream & Chocolate Ganache

Think of this as a very elegant, deconstructed chocolate cake, where the cake pieces are fried, yielding a soft and moist interior and a crisp exterior, much like an old-fashioned donut. While still hot, the chocolatey rounds are tossed in sugar that's been scented with rose oil and clove—two ingredients that can be harsh if used too aggressively but which come alive when warmed, releasing their fragrance without overwhelming your palate. So, while the aroma that hits your nose recalls the Middle East, once you start chewing, you're left with the deep flavor of bittersweet chocolate cake. We serve these donuts with Sherry Diplomat Cream (page 253), which is a pastry cream with whipped cream folded into it, giving it a light, velvety texture, along with a drizzle of Chocolate Ganache (page 253).

SERVES 15

SPECIAL EQUIPMENT:

Candy or other probe-style thermometer

Donut Dough

- 1 ounce (28g) cacao paste or unsweetened baking chocolate
- ⅔ cup (70g) Dutch-processed cocoa powder
- ½ cup (113g) brewed coffee, warm
- ¾ cup plus 2 teaspoons (180g) buttermilk
- 2 teaspoons vanilla extract
- ½ cup (114g) browned butter (see page 238), at room temperature (not melted)
- 1 cup plus 1 tablespoon (210g) granulated sugar
- 3 eggs, at room temperature, yolks and whites separated
- 1 cup plus 2 tablespoons (120g) cake flour
- 1¼ cups (145g) einkorn flour
- 1½ cups (170g) all-purpose flour
- 1 teaspoon (6g) baking soda
- 2½ teaspoons (10g) baking powder
- 2 teaspoons (6g) kosher salt

To make the donut dough: In a medium saucepan, add 1 inch of water and place on the stove over high heat until it comes to a boil. Turn off the heat and nest the bowl of a stand mixer in the rim of the pan, making sure the bowl does not touch the water. Add the cacao paste, stirring continuously until melted.

Meanwhile, in a small bowl, combine the cocoa powder and coffee. Add the buttermilk to dissolve the cocoa powder and then add the vanilla extract.

Move the bowl of melted cacao paste to the stand mixer fitted with the paddle attachment. Add the butter and beat on medium speed until smooth, about 3 minutes. Scrape down the sides of the bowl with a spatula, then add the sugar and mix on medium speed until light and fluffy, about 5 minutes. Scrape down the bowl again, then add the cocoa mixture and mix on medium speed until smooth, about 5 minutes. Scrape down the bowl once more, then add the egg yolks and mix on low until just combined. The mixture will look curdled at this point, but it will all come together.

In a medium bowl, add the cake, einkorn, and all-purpose flours, baking soda, baking powder, and salt and whisk to combine. Remove the bowl from the stand mixer and add the dry mixture. Stir with a spatula until about halfway combined.

CONTINUED

Rose-Clove Donuts with Sherry Diplomat Cream & Chocolate Ganache, continued

Chocolate Flour

¼ cup all-purpose flour

2 tablespoons Dutch-processed cocoa powder

Rose-Clove Sugar

2 cups granulated sugar

1¼ teaspoons ground cloves

¼ plus ⅛ teaspoon kosher salt

1 tablespoon plus 1½ teaspoons dried rose petals, ground

¼ plus ⅛ teaspoon rose oil

Grapeseed oil (may substitute any neutral oil) for frying

Sherry Diplomat Cream (see opposite) for serving

Chocolate Ganache (see opposite) for serving

The exact frying time of the donuts depends on the size you've cut the donuts. Because the donuts are so dark, it can be hard to tell when they're done by sight along. I suggest frying one as a tester to establish the proper timing for the rest of the batch.

In another large bowl, add the egg whites and whisk by hand or using a hand mixer until stiff peaks form, about 5 minutes. Using a spatula, gently fold the egg whites into the half-mixed chocolate batter in two batches until completely combined; do not overmix.

Line a baking sheet with plastic wrap, allowing the excess to hang over the sides. Gently and evenly spread out the batter on the prepared sheet pan. Cover with plastic wrap and smooth out the batter a bit more with your hands or a spatula until it's about ¼ inch thick. Chill in the refrigerator for at least 2 hours.

Remove the baking sheet from the refrigerator and cut the dough into 1½-inch squares that weigh between 21 and 22g. If the dough becomes too soft to work with, place in the refrigerator for 10 to 15 minutes, then continue cutting.

To make the chocolate flour: In a small bowl, add the all-purpose flour and cocoa powder and stir to combine. Line two baking sheets with parchment paper and sprinkle lightly with some of the chocolate flour.

Place the cut donuts onto the prepared baking sheets and sprinkle the tops lightly with more chocolate flour to help prevent them from sticking to your hands. If not frying right away, cover and refrigerate until you're ready to fry. Before frying, remove one pan at a time and let sit for 15 minutes or until the donuts come to room temperature.

To make the rose-clove sugar: Place the sugar, cloves, salt, rose petals, and rose oil in a small bowl and stir to combine.

To fry the donuts: In a large, heavy pot fitted with a candy or instant-read thermometer, preheat the oil to 350°F. Line a plate or sheet pan with paper towels. Fry the donuts in batches, making sure not to overcrowd them, for 1½ minutes on one side, then flip and fry for an additional 30 to 40 seconds on the second side. When finished, the donuts should look puffed up on both sides and be cooked through in the middle*. Place on the prepared plate to drain slightly, then add the donuts to a bowl in batches and toss in the rose-clove sugar. Serve the donuts on a platter with side dishes of the sherry diplomat cream and chocolate ganache for dipping.

Sherry Diplomat Cream

MAKES 5 CUPS

2 tablespoons plus 2 teaspoons (22g) cornstarch

⅔ cup (120g) granulated sugar

¼ teaspoon kosher salt

2 cups (455g) whole milk

4 egg yolks, at room temperature

½ teaspoon vanilla extract

1 tablespoon (15g) aged sherry

1 cup plus 2 tablespoons (270g) heavy whipping cream

¼ cup (60g) crème fraîche

In a large bowl, add the cornstarch, sugar, and salt and whisk until combined.

In a medium saucepan over medium heat, gently heat the milk until warm and steaming, about 6 minutes. Meanwhile, add the egg yolks to the bowl with the dry ingredients and whisk to combine. While whisking, slowly add the scalded milk to the egg mixture. Add the egg mixture back into the saucepan and return to the stove over medium heat. Continue to whisk over the heat until it thickens, about 5 minutes. Remove from the heat and add the vanilla extract and sherry. Stir to combine.

Strain the mixture through a fine-mesh strainer or chinois into a bowl. Cover with plastic wrap, pressing it directly onto the surface and refrigerate until completely cooled, 8 hours or overnight.

Just before ready to serve, combine the cream and crème fraîche together in a bowl and whip with a hand mixer or in a stand mixer fitted with the whisk attachment until stiff peaks form. Remove the pastry cream from the refrigerator and gently fold in the whipped cream until fully incorporated, making sure not to overmix.

Chocolate Ganache

MAKES 1 CUP

½ cup (120g) heavy whipping cream

½ cup (80g) finely chopped dark chocolate*

⅛ teaspoon kosher salt

At Bavel, we source from a remarkable local chocolatier, Nicole Trutanich of Bar Au Chocolat, but we also recommend Valrhona or any other high-quality chocolate that's around 70 percent cacao.

In a small saucepan, add just enough water so a bowl nested in the rim does not touch the water. Place the pan on the stove over high heat until it comes to a boil, then decrease the heat to a simmer.

In a separate small saucepan over medium heat, add the cream and heat until bubbles start to form on the outside edge, about 5 minutes.

In a small bowl, add the chocolate and salt. Pour the heated cream over the chocolate and gently stir. Nest the bowl of chocolate and cream in the saucepan with the water and continue to gently stir over the water bath until the chocolate is completely melted, about 2 minutes.

If the ganache is being made a few hours ahead of time, add the ganache to a preheated thermos, cover, and reserve until serving.

Coconut Tapioca

I love boba! It's true, and it also happens to be the name of a boba place I used to frequent near my house in L.A. When boba first started becoming popular here in the late '90s, I didn't like it. It was gooey, squishy, and lightly sweet, and I didn't understand the obsession. But once you've had it a few times, that texture becomes something you crave. This recipe began with the idea of a coconut rice pudding, but then I thought, what if I did a coconut tapioca instead? We cook the tapioca pearls gently, so they retain a bit of that bobalike bounce and chew. And because tapioca soaks up so much water, even though it's in a rich mixture of milk, cream, and coconut cream, it's actually an incredibly light, refreshing dessert. We top it with a golden drizzle of cane sugar saffron syrup and pair it with a lacy coconut tuile for a delicate crunch and to echo the buttery flavor of the saffron.

SERVES 10

1⅔ cups (400g) cold water, divided
½ cup plus 1 tablespoon (95g) small pearl tapioca*
1 cup plus 2 tablespoons (250g) coconut cream
1½ cups (350g) whole milk
⅔ cup (150g) heavy whipping cream
½ cup (100g) granulated sugar
¼ teaspoon kosher salt
Saffron Syrup (page 258) for serving
Coconut Tuile (page 258) for serving

Bob's Red Mill is our preferred brand.

In a small bowl, combine approximately half of the cold water and the tapioca. Let sit at room temperature, uncovered, until the water is absorbed by the tapioca, about 20 to 30 minutes.

In a medium saucepan over medium-low heat, add the remaining water, the coconut cream, milk, whipping cream, sugar, and salt and gently stir with a spatula to combine. Let the pan sit over the heat until the sugar and salt have dissolved and the mixture starts to steam and bubble on the sides of the pan, about 15 minutes. Make sure not to let the mixture come to a full boil. Add the soaked tapioca to the saucepan and gently combine with a spatula. Continue to cook over low heat, occasionally gently scraping the bottom of the pan with the spatula to avoid clumping, until the tapioca pearls start to float to the top and are chewy but still have a slight bite, 10 to 12 minutes.

Fill a large bowl with ice and nest a smaller bowl on top of the ice; set aside. Remove the saucepan from the heat and pour the mixture into the nested bowl. Let it sit, uncovered, for 20 minutes, gently mixing every 5 minutes to prevent a skin from forming on top. Once cooled, cover the bowl with plastic wrap, pressing it directly onto the surface of the tapioca so a film does not form, and refrigerate until ready to use. The tapioca can be made 1 day in advance but it is best served the day it's made.

When ready to serve, place ½ cup of the tapioca in a small dish or coupe glass with 2 teaspoons of the saffron syrup drizzled on top and one coconut tuile on the side.

CONTINUED

Saffron Syrup

MAKES 2 CUPS

¼ teaspoon saffron threads
¾ cup plus 2 tablespoons (175g)
  boiling water
1¼ cups (250g) cane sugar

In a small saucepan, combine the saffron and boiling water. Let the saffron bloom in the water for 5 minutes. Add the sugar and place the saucepan over medium heat. Bring to a boil and cook for 3 minutes. Let cool and store in an airtight container in the refrigerator for up to 3 days.

Coconut Tuile

MAKES ABOUT 36 TUILES

7 tablespoons (50g) all-purpose flour
½ cup (50g) unsweetened shredded
  coconut
¼ cup (65g) egg whites (from about
  2 eggs)
½ cup (100g) granulated sugar
¼ teaspoon kosher salt
½ teaspoon vanilla extract
5 tablespoons (70g) unsalted butter,
  melted

In a small bowl, combine the flour and coconut; set aside.

In a medium bowl, add the egg whites, sugar, salt, and vanilla extract and whisk until incorporated. In a slow and steady stream, add the butter while whisking. Add the flour and coconut mixture and, using a spatula, fold gently to combine; do not overmix. Cover with plastic wrap and refrigerate for 4 hours or up to 2 days.

Preheat the oven to 325°F. Line two baking sheets with silicone mats. Cut a circular stencil from a plastic container lid or other circle that is 3½ inches in diameter. (The top of an ice cream pint works best. Simply cut out the center, then cut down the outer edge to get a flat, circular stencil.)

Remove the batter from the refrigerator. Put the stencil on the prepared pan. Using a small offset spatula, swipe a very thin layer of batter to fill the circle. Repeat to make as many tuiles as will fit without crowding. Refrigerate the batter between baking batches.

Bake for 10 minutes, or until light golden brown. Remove the baking sheet from the oven and swipe underneath the tuiles with the offset spatula so they don't stick while cooling. Let cool on the baking sheet. Repeat with the second batch. Store in an airtight container at room temperature for up to 3 days.

Peach Cobbler

There are three basic components to this dessert—peaches, ice cream, and cake—but if you had to pick one thing that could really stand on its own, it's the cake. Technically a financier, this molded almond flour–based cake is a lightly modified version of a recipe by Craig Thornton of the L.A. supper club Wolvesmouth. I've made many different financiers in my day, but I tried Craig's version once, and it just blew my mind. As one of my pastry chefs accurately described it, "it's like a madeleine with more oomph, with an incredibly buttery, almost creamy inside and a crispy shell outside." It's so good that I built an entire dessert around it.

What I love about this elevated version of a peach cobbler is that each element is cooked separately, so you have a lot more control over the cooking of the peaches. Instead of baking them with the cake, they're lightly sautéed in a peach syrup, so the texture and flavor are more like a great fresh peach. If you're going to make the whole cobbler, do as we do at Bavel and dust the dessert with the Baharat Spice Blend (page 34). If you are going to make the cakes on their own, as I regularly do for my daughter (they are her favorite treats in the world), then you would add the baharat spice to the batter for an incredibly fragrant financier.

SERVES 12

Note: I highly recommend weighing the ingredients for the financier recipe. However, I created the cup measurements that are slightly altered for ease. If you are well-versed in measurements, you will notice that the two don't line up with each other; this is purposeful. The cup measurements were altered so it looks like a recipe that belongs on planet earth.

Financiers

MAKES 12

SPECIAL EQUIPMENT:

Twelve 2½- to 3-inch aluminum financier molds

Ice cream maker

Batter

½ cup (50g) almond flour

¼ cup (25g) cake flour

3 tablespoons (25g) all-purpose flour, plus more for dusting the molds

1¼ cups (147g) confectioners' sugar

2 teaspoons Baharat Spice Blend (page 34); optional

1 teaspoon (3g) fleur de sel

9 tablespoons (125g) browned butter (see page 238)

⅔ cup (125g) egg whites, at room temperature

To make the batter: In a large bowl, sift together the almond, cake, and all-purpose flours, sugar; and spice blend (if using). Gently stir in the salt.

In a small saucepan, warm the butter over very low heat, while stirring, until just melted and warm. If you heat up the brown butter over any higher heat, it will burn. Set aside.

In the bowl of a stand mixer fitted with a whisk attachment, add the egg whites and vanilla extract. Beat on medium speed until foamy, like a jacuzzi circa 1985, about 5 minutes. Then add the bowl of dry ingredients and mix on low speed until thoroughly

CONTINUED

2 teaspoons (3g) vanilla extract
(Tahitian preferred)
Butter for greasing the molds

3 to 4 large peaches
¼ cup Peach Syrup (recipe below),
warm
Ricotta Ice Cream (page 262)
Baharat Spice Blend (page 34)
for serving

combined. Once fully incorporated, very slowly drizzle in the brown butter on medium-low speed and mix until the butter is fully incorporated and disappears. You will need to scrape down the sides and bottom of the bowl multiple times to make sure the butter is as evenly absorbed as possible. Transfer the batter to an airtight container and refrigerate for at least 6 hours or up to 1 week.

Butter and lightly flour the financier molds, tapping out any excess flour. Place the molds on a sheet pan and chill in the refrigerator for at least 20 minutes or until you're ready to fill them.

Preheat the oven to 350°F. Remove the batter from the refrigerator and let it come to room temperature. Fill the chilled molds two-thirds full. Bake for 18 to 25 minutes, depending on your mold size, until golden and a bump has formed in the center. Remove the molds from the oven and let cool for just 2 minutes before removing the financiers from the molds. If they cool all the way, they will stick to the mold because of the high sugar content.

To prepare the peaches: Slice each large peach into eighteen to twenty ¼-inch-thick slices and set aside. In a medium sauté pan over medium-high heat, add ¼ cup of the peach syrup and cook until the syrup begins to bubble. Decrease the heat to medium-low and add the peach slices in a single layer. Sauté for 30 seconds on each side. Remove from the heat.

When ready to serve, add five peach slices and 1 teaspoon of the peach syrup into the bottom of a shallow bowl or plate. Add 1 financier, a scoop of the ice cream, and a generous dusting of the spice blend. Serve immediately.

Peach Syrup

MAKES 2 CUPS

1¾ cups (375g) cane sugar
¼ cup (67g) crème de peche liqueur
1 cup (250g) moscato
1 teaspoon citric acid

In a medium saucepan over high heat, combine the sugar, liqueur, moscato, and citric acid. Bring to a boil and cook for 3 minutes. Remove from the heat and let cool. Store in an airtight container in the refrigerator for up to 2 weeks. Leftover syrup is a delicious sweetener for iced tea. Woo hoo!

CONTINUED

Ricotta Ice Cream

MAKES ABOUT 1 QUART

1 cup (227g) whole milk
½ cup (120g) heavy whipping cream
1 cup (200g) granulated sugar
6 egg yolks
2 cups (453g) whole milk ricotta
½ cup (115g) buttermilk
½ teaspoon freshly squeezed
  lemon juice
¼ teaspoon kosher salt

Combine the milk, cream, and ¾ cup (150g) of the sugar in a medium saucepan and cook over medium heat, stirring occasionally, until the mixture just begins to bubble. Remove from the heat.

Meanwhile, in a large bowl, whisk together the egg yolks with the remaining ¼ cup (50g) sugar. Slowly pour the warm cream mixture into the yolks while whisking constantly until fully incorporated. Then pour the whole mixture back into the saucepan and cook over very low heat, stirring continuously with a spatula, until the mixture is thick enough to coat the back of a spoon, about 10 minutes.

Meanwhile, in a large bowl, combine the ricotta and buttermilk. When the ice cream base has thickened, pour it through a very-fine-mesh strainer or chinois into the bowl with the ricotta and buttermilk and stir to combine.

Cover the bowl with plastic wrap, pressing it onto the surface of the ice cream base to avoid forming a skin, and refrigerate until very cold, 8 hours or overnight.

Just before churning, stir in the lemon juice. Transfer the mixture to an ice cream maker and churn according to the manufacturer's instructions. Store in an airtight container in the freezer for up to 1 week.

Date-Walnut Tart

This tart might be the most reminiscent of a traditional Middle Eastern dessert we have at Bavel, but a somewhat similar version of it actually first appeared on the menu at Bestia. When I started serving it, Ori said I should save it for our forthcoming Middle Eastern restaurant, but I just couldn't help myself. The base is similar to my crostata dough but with the slight sour tang of yogurt to balance out the sweetness of the dates, and it comes with a Fig Leaf Crème Anglaise (page 267), made from the snipped-off fig leaves surrounding Bestia's courtyard. But for me, what really makes this dessert is the combination of the salted brown butter and date vinegar, a genius pairing that I can't take credit for. There's a restaurant in L.A. called Hatchet Hall where chef Brian Dunsmoor will sometimes serve an appetizer of warm dates that have been sautéed in butter, splashed with a bit of date vinegar, and sprinkled with Maldon salt. It's a perfect little bite that inspired the finishing touches of this dessert. We sauce up the plate beneath the tart with some double-salted brown butter and vinegar, coaxing out the flavor of the walnuts and providing the bright acidity that dates crave.

MAKES 2 LARGE TARTS; SERVES 18

Tart Dough (page 265), frozen

Date Cream (page 265)

¾ to 1 cup Walnut Cream (page 266)

Butter, at room temperature, for brushing

Cane sugar for dusting

1 cup plus 2 tablespoons melted brown butter (see page 238), with 1 teaspoon kosher salt whisked in

3 tablespoons date vinegar

Fig Leaf Crème Anglaise (page 267)

Preheat the oven to 375°F. Line a baking sheet with parchment paper.

To assemble each tart: Take out two of the frozen sheets of dough and place them side by side. Thinly spread half of the date cream on one sheet. Then thinly spread about ½ cup of the walnut cream on the other sheet as if you are making a peanut butter and jelly sandwich. Make sure to leave a border of about ¼ inch on all four edges to seal. Sandwich the two sheets, pressing the two cream sides together. Crimp around all sides with a fork to seal. Cut three small ¼-inch slits on top of the tart. These vents will allow steam to escape and prevent the tart from becoming domed.

Brush the top with butter and lightly dust with an even layer of sugar.

Place the assembled tart on the prepared baking sheet. Bake for 17 to 18 minutes, until golden brown.

Serve warm, either just out of the oven or reheated; this is also delicious at room temperature. When ready to serve, cut the tart into nine individual pieces. Drizzle 1 tablespoon of the salted brown butter and ½ teaspoon of the date vinegar onto each plate. Top with a warmed piece of the tart. Serve with 2 tablespoons of the crème anglaise on the side.

CONTINUED

Tart Dough

MAKES 2 LARGE TARTS

1⅓ cups (155g) all-purpose flour,
  plus more for dusting
⅓ cup (32g) Sonora wheat flour (may
  substitute whole-wheat pastry flour)
⅛ teaspoon baking soda
½ teaspoon kosher salt
½ cup (113g) butter, frozen and cubed
½ cup (113g) Yogurt (page 81); may
  substitute store-bought whole milk
  Greek yogurt

To make the dough: In a medium bowl, add the all-purpose and Sonora flours, baking soda, and salt. Whisk to combine. Add the dry mixture to a food processor and then add the butter. Pulse the butter until the mixture resembles coarse meal. Add the yogurt and pulse three or four times until mostly combined.

Dump the flour-yogurt mixture into a medium bowl and gently mix with a fork. If the dough seems too dry and crumbly, add up to 3 tablespoons ice-cold water (1 tablespoon at a time), until the dough is hydrated but not sticky. Finish kneading the dough by hand in the bowl until it just comes together; do not overknead.

Line a work surface with four pieces of plastic wrap. Divide the dough into four even portions and cover with the plastic wrap. Smash each piece of the wrapped dough into a round disk. Store in the refrigerator for at least 2 hours. The dough can be made up to 2 days in advance or stored in the freezer for up to 2 weeks.

Remove the dough from the refrigerator or freezer and let sit until pliable but not room temperature. Line a baking sheet with parchment paper. Lightly dust a work surface with flour and roll out each piece of dough into a rectangle about 15 by 10 inches. The dough will be very thin, but this is what you want. Transfer one portion of dough onto the baking sheet, then add a layer of parchment paper or plastic wrap to protect it, and continue stacking the dough, with parchment or plastic separating each layer. Wrap the whole baking sheet in plastic wrap and place in the freezer until ready to use.

Date Cream

MAKES ABOUT ½ CUP

¼ cup (55g) heavy whipping cream
¼ teaspoon vanilla extract
Pinch of kosher salt
½ cup (140g) firmly packed pitted
  soft dates

In a small saucepan over low heat, combine the cream, vanilla extract, and salt and cook until small bubbles form around the outside edges of the pan, about 3 minutes. Remove the pan from the heat and add the dates, allowing the heated cream to soften the dates. Let sit for 3 minutes. Add the hot date-cream mixture to a food processor or blender and puree until smooth.

While still warm, press the mixture through a fine-mesh sieve or tamis to remove the skins, if desired.

CONTINUED

Walnut Cream

MAKES ABOUT 1½ CUPS

1 cup (100g) walnuts
1 cup (115g) confectioners' sugar
½ cup (113g) unsalted butter,
　at room temperature
1 egg
1 egg yolk
¼ cup (35g) cornstarch
1 tablespoon (15g) walnut oil
1 tablespoon (15g) Grand Marnier
　or apple brandy
1 cup (170g) Pastry Cream
　(recipe below)

Note: This yields ½ cup more walnut cream than you'll need for this tart, but it's a versatile ingredient. Spread the extra on a halved croissant or brioche, bake at 350°F for 10 to 12 minutes, and enjoy.

In a food processor, add the walnuts and ½ cup (58g) of the sugar. Pulse until the walnuts are coarsely ground and the mixture resembles cornmeal.

In a stand mixer fitted with the paddle attachment, add the remaining ½ cup (57g) sugar and the butter. Cream on medium-high speed until fluffy, 5 to 7 minutes. Add the remaining ingredients in the following order, stopping to scrape down the bowl of the mixer before adding the next batch of ingredients: first the egg and yolk, then the cornstarch and walnut mixture, and then the oil and Grand Marnier. Finally, gently fold in the pastry cream with a spatula.

Pastry Cream

MAKES ABOUT 1 CUP

1 cup (227g) whole milk
½ vanilla bean, halved and
　seeds removed
¼ cup (50g) granulated sugar
⅛ teaspoon kosher salt
1 tablespoon (10g) cornstarch
1 egg
2 tablespoons (30g) unsalted butter

In a medium saucepan over medium heat, add the milk and vanilla bean seeds and pod and heat until scalding, about 5 minutes.

In a medium bowl, add the sugar, salt, cornstarch, and egg and whisk to combine. Very slowly add the heated milk to the egg mixture while whisking continuously. Return the mixture to the saucepan and cook over medium heat, continuing to whisk, until thick. Look for big, long-lasting bubbles. Remove the pan from the heat and add the butter. Strain the mixture through a fine-mesh sieve. Let cool to room temperature before using.

Fig Leaf Crème Anglaise

MAKES 2¼ CUPS

10 medium (50g) fig leaves, washed, stemmed, and membranes stripped out*

⅓ cup (70g) granulated sugar

5 egg yolks

1½ cups (340g) heavy whipping cream

½ cup (114g) whole milk

⅛ teaspoon kosher salt

The membranes are the large white veins running through the fig leaves. Removing these veins prevents the crème anglaise from becoming bitter and curdling when heated.

Add the fig leaves and sugar to a food processor. Grind thoroughly until a green paste forms.

In a medium bowl, beat the egg yolks until smooth, then set aside.

In a medium saucepan over medium heat, add the cream, milk, fig leaf–sugar mixture, and salt. Cook, stirring often, until scalding, 6 to 8 minutes. Remove the pan from the heat and strain through a fine-mesh sieve, pressing out all the liquid with the back of a spoon.

In a very slow and steady stream, add all of the heated fig leaf mixture to the beaten egg yolks while whisking continuously to temper. Then pour the whole mixture back into the saucepan and cook over very low heat, stirring continuously with a spatula, until it's thick enough to coat the back of a spoon, or nappe. Strain the mixture through the fine-mesh sieve a second time and cover with a piece of plastic wrap touching the surface of the cream to prevent it from forming a skin. Let cool to room temperature and then store in the refrigerator for up to 3 days.

Persian Mulberry Pudding Cake

The first time I had a Persian mulberry was when the bar manager at Bestia brought me some from his mother-in-law's garden. At first glance, they didn't look like much; they looked like what we now call grandpa blackberries—small and delicate with a few tiny fibers on them like errant whiskers. But once I had tried them, I couldn't get the flavor out of my head. They were juicy and fragrant, with a deeper berry flavor than anything I'd experienced before. You can make this cake with any combination of berries—raspberries, blackberries, huckleberries, blueberries—but the intensity of a Persian mulberry eclipses them all.

The allure of this dessert is in the juxtaposition of that pungent, deep berry flavor with a superlight, airy chiffon cake. The berry is incorporated in two ways: as a puree that soaks into the cake and as a mash that retains the textural berry bite. The cake itself is extremely versatile—in summer, I split it open and pile it with vanilla whipped cream and gently macerated strawberries for an exquisitely light strawberry shortcake. It also goes well with any kind of citrus curd or even frosted with a light chocolate buttercream.

MAKES 1 CAKE; SERVES 8

SPECIAL EQUIPMENT:

10-inch angel food cake pan with removable bottom and with feet; must be aluminum— nonstick will not work.

5 eggs, whites and yolks separated, at room temperature

1 teaspoon freshly squeezed lemon juice

1½ cups (300g) granulated sugar

2¾ cups (280g) cake flour

2 teaspoons baking powder

¼ teaspoon baking soda

1½ teaspoons kosher salt

¾ cup (150g) grapeseed oil

1 cup (230g) buttermilk, at room temperature

2 teaspoons vanilla extract

Berry Puree (page 271)

Berry Mash (page 271)

Whipped Crème Fraîche (page 271)

Preheat the oven to 350°F.

In the bowl of a stand mixer fitted with the whisk attachment, add the egg whites and lemon juice and whisk on medium speed. When the egg whites start to form bubbles and begin to look frothy, like an inviting bubble bath, add ¼ cup (50g) of the sugar. Continue to whisk on medium speed until stiff peaks form and the mixture is glossy and shiny, about 12 minutes.

Meanwhile, in a large bowl, sift together the flour, baking powder, baking soda, salt, and the remaining 1¼ cups (250g) sugar.

In a separate medium bowl, add the oil, buttermilk, vanilla extract, and egg yolks. Whisk to combine. Add the wet ingredients to the large bowl with the dry ingredients. Using the whisk, fold together the dry and wet ingredients until just combined.

Using the whisk, gently fold in one-third of the egg white mixture, being mindful not to overmix. Add the remaining egg whites in thirds until everything is folded together. Finish combining with a few folds with a spatula.

CONTINUED

Persian Mulberry Pudding Cake, continued

Add the batter to the cake pan; do not grease the pan. Bake for 45 to 50 minutes, until the top is golden-brown and a toothpick comes out with moist crumbs. Remove from the oven and flip the pan upside down onto a baking sheet. Let cool for about 2 hours. Remove the cake from the pan by dragging a knife or large offset spatula around the outside edge, then push the removable bottom out of the ringed edge of the pan.

Using a serrated bread knife, trim the top of the cake so it is flat. Then cut the cake into three layers. The top layer can be fairly thin, about 1 inch thick, leaving enough cake remaining to split into two very thick layers.

Wash and dry the pan thoroughly. Then line the pan with four layers of plastic wrap. Place the bottom thick layer of cake into the lined pan. Pour one-third of the berry puree over the bottom layer of the cake and top with half of the berry mash. Place the middle thick layer of cake on top, then pour another one-third of the puree on top of the middle layer and top with the other half of the berry mash. Finally, place the thinner top layer of cake on top and pour the remaining one-third of the berry puree over the layer. Fully wrap the built cake in plastic wrap and chill in the refrigerator overnight.

When ready to serve, remove the cake from the refrigerator. Unwrap the plastic and carefully remove the cake from the pan. Slice while still cold and serve a slice on a plate with a dollop of the crème fraîche.

Berry Puree

MAKES ENOUGH FOR 1 CAKE

SPECIAL
EQUIPMENT:

*Immersion
blender*

2⅔ cups (1 pound / 455g) fresh
   raspberries

½ cup plus 2 tablespoons (136g) water

1¼ cups plus 2 tablespoons (278g)
   granulated sugar

3 tablespoons (45g) raspberry liqueur
   (may substitute blackberry liqueur,
   creme de cassis, or fraise des bois)

2⅔ cups (1 pound / 455g) fresh
   blackberries

2⅔ cups (1 pound / 455g) fresh
   Persian mulberries

In a medium saucepan, combine the raspberries with ¼ cup plus 1 tablespoon (68g) of the water, ½ cup plus 1 tablespoon (114g) of the sugar, and 2 tablespoons (23g) of the liqueur. Cook over low heat until the sugar has dissolved and the fruit is slightly broken down, about 5 minutes. Remove the pan from the heat and blend with an immersion blender. Strain through a fine-mesh sieve or tamis and set aside.

In a separate medium saucepan, add the blackberries with the remaining ¼ cup plus 1 tablespoon (68g) water, ½ cup plus 1 tablespoon (114g) of the sugar, and the remaining 2 tablespoons (23g) liqueur. Cook over low heat until the sugar has dissolved and the blackberries start to get lighter in color, about 10 minutes. Remove from heat and blend with the immersion blender. Strain through the fine-mesh strainer or tamis and set aside.

Add the mulberries and the remaining ¼ cup (50g) sugar to a blender and puree.

In a bowl, stir together 2 cups of the raspberry puree, 2 cups of the blackberry puree, and 2 cups of the mulberry puree. If the puree is made in advance, store it in an airtight container in the refrigerator for up to 1 day. Alternatively, the puree can be stored in the freezer for up to 1 week. Defrost at room temperature before pouring over the cake.

Berry Mash

MAKES ENOUGH FOR 1 CAKE

1 cup (one 6-ounce container)
   blueberries

1 cup (one 6-ounce container)
   raspberries

1 cup (one 6-ounce container)
   blackberries

½ cup plus 3 tablespoons (137g)
   granulated sugar

2 tablespoons (30g) raspberry
   liqueur (may substitute any
   other dark berry liqueur)

In a large saucepan, add the berries, sugar, and liqueur. Place on the stove over medium heat and cook, stirring with a spatula, until the sugar has dissolved and the raspberries have broken down, about 4 minutes. Remove from the heat and, using a fork, smash the blackberries in the pan.

Note: If you are using a scale to measure, you will need 550g total of berries. You may also use any combination of berries that you prefer.

Whipped Crème Fraîche

MAKES ENOUGH FOR 1 CAKE

1 cup (240g) crème fraîche
2 cups (480g) heavy whipping cream

In a stand mixer fitted with the whisk attachment, add the crème fraîche and cream and beat on medium-high speed until soft peaks form.

Spiced Camp Cake

It was the beginning of October, and we finally had our first couple of cool fall days in L.A. Ori, Saffron, and I were due to go camping with some friends. Whenever we camp, I'm always in charge of desserts for the group. I had planned on making something with late-summer plums or peaches, but as soon as that first cold snap hit, I felt a rush of fall and wanted to do something with apples. I decided to come up with a recipe for apple cake that would forgo the usual moistening agents, like buttermilk, milk, or water, in favor of a recipe just loaded with fruit.

I played around with the numbers on paper for a while until I had a recipe that was basically just thinly sliced apples tossed in the dry ingredients. You couldn't even really call it a batter. I remember I made a test batch and said to Valerie, a member of my pastry team, "This is most likely going to go in the trash." It just looked like a bunch of apples coated in dry cake mix. I put it in the oven, came back ten minutes later, and you could see—all of a sudden—the cake had puffed up around the apples. I said, "Wait; this could work." Not only did it work, but it was the type of cake that was delicious on first bite and became even better and more moist over time.

What makes this cake work is the huge amount of fruit that releases its moisture at the same time the batter heats up, providing the steam and elevation needed for it to rise. The result is the sort of beautiful, moist spice cake that you could eat plain or serve with vanilla whipped cream and our salted brown butter–date vinegar blend (see page 263) at an elegant dinner party. It's delicious still warm, fresh out of the oven, but I like it even more the next day, gently heated on a piece of aluminum foil over a campfire.

Note: Part of the secret to this cake is thinly slicing the pears or apples about ⅛ inch thick with a knife or more quickly with a mandoline. The ultra-thin fruit floats in the batter instead of sinking to the bottom, so the batter puffs up around it, and the fruit gets distributed evenly, almost like ribbons, throughout the cake.

SERVES 8 TO 10

Butter for greasing the baking dish

2 tablespoons cane sugar

2¾ teaspoons ground cinnamon

1 teaspoon baking soda

1½ teaspoons kosher salt

1 cup (115g) Sonora wheat flour (may substitute any whole-wheat flour)

1 cup (115g) all-purpose flour

½ cup (60g) packed almond flour

1 cup (200g) packed muscovado sugar (may substitute light brown sugar)

¾ cup (150g) granulated sugar

Preheat the oven to 350°F. Grease a 9 by 13-inch baking dish with butter.

In a small bowl, combine the cane sugar and ¾ teaspoon of the cinnamon, then set aside.

In a large bowl, add the remaining 2 teaspoons cinnamon; baking soda; salt; Sonora, all-purpose, and almond flours; and the muscovado and granulated sugars. Whisk to combine until no lumps of brown sugar remain.

In a separate large bowl, add the pears and lemon juice. Stir gently to combine.

CONTINUED

2⅔ cups (about 4) thinly sliced pears; may substitute 4 cups (about 6) sweet yet tart apples* (see Variation)

2 tablespoons freshly squeezed lemon juice

½ cup (100g) grapeseed oil

2 eggs, at room temperature

1 teaspoon vanilla extract

¼ teaspoon almond extract

vanilla whipped cream for serving

Look for Warren, Taylor's Gold, or any creamy, floral pear. Do not use Asian or Bosc pears; they are too watery and don't have enough flavor for this cake. If using apples, look for a sweet yet tart variety, like Jonagold, Honeycrisp, or Pink Lady.

In another small bowl, add the oil, eggs, and vanilla and almond extracts. Whisk to combine. Pour over the pears. Fold gently to combine. Slowly fold in the dry ingredients until just combined; do not overmix. It is normal for some of the pear slices to break into pieces.

Add the batter to the prepared baking dish. Evenly sprinkle the cinnamon-sugar mixture on top of the batter.

Bake for 30 to 40 minutes, until a crust forms on top and a toothpick inserted into the middle comes out with no wet crumbs. Let cool for 30 minutes before slicing. Serve a slice of cake on a plate with vanilla whipped cream.

Variation: If using apples instead of pears, follow the recipe directions except for the following: use 1 tablespoon lemon juice; reduce the amount of muscovado sugar by 2 tablespoons (25g); and use ⅔ cup (135g) granulated sugar.

Honey-Nougat Glace

Nougat is a very typical Middle Eastern candy that's usually made with rose or orange blossom water, nuts, and dried fruit and is sweetened with honey. When I was growing up, my dad, who loved nougat, would put wrapped versions in little candy dishes, like the ones you would find filled with butterscotches and peppermints in other American homes. He could never understand why my sister and I would prefer something like Skittles—fake-dyed, processed junk—to this floral, pistachio-packed delicacy. And so, those candies would sit in the same bowl for years, until they became petrified objects of curiosity.

As an adult, I came to understand the beauty of those little candies, and I wanted to create a dessert inspired by them for Bavel, so I decided on a nougat terrine. The first version I made was more like a molded semifreddo—a semi-frozen cream dessert made without an ice cream maker. But in my second version, which uses an ice cream maker, the base comes out super silky and almost marshmallowy, reminiscent of the texture of real nougat and chock-full of candied fruit and nuts.

SERVES 8

SPECIAL EQUIPMENT:

12 by 3¼-inch terrine mold with a removable bottom (optional)

Candy or other probe-style thermometer

Ice cream maker (optional)

1½ cups plus 3 tablespoons (400g) egg whites

¼ cup plus 1½ tablespoons (66g) superfine sugar

3 tablespoons plus 1 teaspoon (66g) glucose (may substitute corn syrup)

½ cup (147g) honey

Rounded ⅛ teaspoon kosher salt

¼ cup (40g) Amaro Nonino

2 tablespoons (19g) orange blossom water

2⅓ cups (533g) heavy whipping cream

½ cup plus 1 tablespoon (135g) crème fraîche

Pine Nut Nougatine (page 276)

Candied Kumquats (page 276)

If making the ice cream version, line the terrine mold with plastic wrap or parchment paper. Store in the freezer for a minimum of 30 minutes or as long as you like.

For either version: In a stand mixer fitted with the whisk attachment, whip the egg whites on medium speed until foamy, soft peaks form, about 2½ minutes.

In a small saucepan fitted with a candy thermometer, combine the sugar, glucose, honey, and salt and heat over medium heat to 250°F.

Increase the speed of the stand mixer to high and pour the sugar mixture in all at once while the mixer remains on high. Scrape as much of the sugar mixture out of the saucepan as you can with a spatula into the bowl. Mix until very fluffy, about 5 minutes. Decrease the mixer speed to low and continue mixing until the outside of the bowl becomes room temperature, 5 to 8 minutes. Remove the bowl from the mixer stand and nest it in a bowl of ice water. Let the mixture cool, whisking it occasionally by hand, until it becomes as cold as possible, about 30 minutes.

In a separate medium bowl, combine the amaro, orange blossom water, cream, and crème fraîche.

To make the glace using the ice cream method: Gently stir the cream mixture into the egg white mixture, then transfer the combined mixtures to an ice cream maker and churn according to the manufacturer's instructions.

CONTINUED

Honey-Nougat Glace, continued

Remove the frozen prepared mold from the freezer. Evenly scatter one-third of the chopped nougatine, then one-third of the kumquats over the bottom of the mold. Fill the mold with ice cream about halfway full. Top with another one-third of the nougatine scattered evenly, then one-third of the kumquats. Add the remaining ice cream mixture, spread evenly, and top with the remaining nougatine and kumquats. Cover with plastic wrap and store in the freezer until fully solidified and firm, at least 6 hours or up to 1 week.

Serve, remove the mold from the freezer and slice into 1-inch-thick pieces. Serve immediately.

To make the glace using the semifreddo method: Transfer the chilled egg mixture to another bowl and refrigerate. Mix the cream mixture in the stand mixer on medium speed for about 5 minutes, until it holds soft-medium peaks. Fold the whipped cream mixture into the chilled egg white and sugar mixture.

Line the bottom of a 9 by 13-inch baking dish with plastic wrap. Scatter the chopped nougatine and kumquats evenly over the bottom of the dish. Add the whipped cream–egg white mixture, then cover again with plastic wrap and freeze for at least 6 hours or overnight. Once frozen solid, cut into squares and serve with the nougat and kumquat side up.

Pine Nut Nougatine

MAKES ABOUT ½ CUP

½ cup (100g) granulated sugar
Pinch of kosher salt
¼ teaspoon vanilla extract
1 teaspoon (10g) glucose (may substitute corn syrup)
Very full ⅓ cup (50g) toasted pine nuts

In a small saucepan over medium heat, add the sugar, salt, vanilla extract, and glucose. Add just enough water until the mixture looks like wet sand; using a wet brush, brush down any sugar crystals that begin to form on the side of the pan. Cook until golden brown and caramelized. Remove from the heat and add the pine nuts. Spread the mixture over a silicone baking mat. Let cool and then chop into ¼-inch pieces. Store at room temperature in an airtight container for up to 3 days.

Candied Kumquats

MAKES 1 CUP

½ cup granulated sugar
½ cup water
1 teaspoon glucose (may substitute corn syrup)
½ cup quartered and seeded kumquats (may substitute mandarinquats)

In a medium saucepan over medium-high heat, combine the sugar, water, and glucose. Bring to a boil. Add the kumquats, decrease the heat to a low simmer, and cook until translucent, about 30 minutes. Store in the refrigerator in an airtight container for up to 1 month.

Saffron–Meyer Lemon Bars

Lemon bars are delicious, but they're trickier to make than they seem. Depending on the lemon, even the most perfectly baked lemon bars can become metallic tasting or more one-note sour than sweet. As I've become more knowledgeable about citrus, I've learned that the secret to a great lemon bar is using the right fruit; that is why I like to use only Meyer lemons or Bearss limes (sometimes called Persian limes) or even Key limes. Meyer lemons are a cross between a lemon and a mandarin and taste just like a sweet lemon candy. Bearss or Persian limes are a cross between a Key lime and a lemon and taste like the best margarita you've ever had. When used in baked goods, both varieties have a pure citrus sweetness with a less metallic overtone than a standard grocery store lemon. (If neither is available, try for Eureka lemons, which are also very lovely and available most of the year.) We steep a few saffron threads in the lemon juice before mixing, which elevates this simple, nostalgic dessert to something really beautiful.

MAKES ABOUT 24 BARS

Dough

2 cups (230g) all-purpose flour

¾ cup (85g) whole-wheat pastry flour

½ cup (100g) granulated sugar

1½ teaspoons kosher salt

1 cup (227g) butter, frozen and cubed, plus more for greasing the pan

1½ teaspoons vanilla extract

¼ cup (55g) heavy whipping cream

2 egg yolks

Filling

1 cup (225g) freshly squeezed Meyer lemon juice

2 tablespoons (30g) sparkling white or sparkling rosé wine

Medium pinch (about 15 large strands) of saffron threads (omit if using lime juice)

2 tablespoons lightly packed Meyer lemon zest (omit if using lime juice)

3 cups (600g) granulated sugar

¾ cup plus 1 tablespoon (96g) all-purpose flour

6 eggs

2 egg yolks

To make the dough: In a medium bowl, add the all-purpose and pastry flours, sugar, and salt and whisk to combine. Add the mixture to a food processor. With the food processor running, add the butter and process until it is incorporated and the mixture resembles coarse meal, similar to sand.

In a small bowl, add the vanilla extract, cream, and egg yolks and whisk to combine.

Add the cream mixture to the food processor. Place the lid back on and process until a dough ball forms.

Transfer the dough to a silicone baking mat or a cold, clean work surface. Taking about ¼ cup of the dough at a time, smear it across the mat or work surface with the heel of your hand to fully incorporate all of the ingredients. Repeat with the remaining dough until the entire mixture has been smeared on the mat. Using a scraper, gather all of the smeared dough into a ball.

Reserve about 2 tablespoons of the dough at room temperature to patch up any cracks or holes after blind baking so the filling won't spill out.

Butter a 9 by 13-inch pan. Line only the bottom of the pan with parchment paper and butter the top of the paper. Using your fingers, press the dough into the bottom of the pan and about 1 inch up all four sides. Cover with plastic wrap and place the pan (plus reserved dough for patching if not baking the same day) in the freezer for at least 30 minutes or up to 1 week.

CONTINUED

When ready to bake, preheat the oven to 350°F. Bake for 5 minutes, then decrease the temperature to 300°F and bake for an additional 50 minutes to 1 hour, until the top is a very even deep golden brown. Remove from the oven and let cool for at least 10 minutes. Bring the reserved dough to room temperature and use it to patch up any cracks, holes, or slumped spaces on the sides.

To make the filling: In a small bowl, combine the lemon juice and wine. Add the saffron threads and let bloom for at least 15 minutes.

In a separate large bowl, rub the lemon zest and sugar together with your fingers until fully incorporated and fragrant. Add the flour and whisk thoroughly to prevent any clumps. Whisk in the saffron juice mixture to combine. Add the eggs and yolks, whisking until thoroughly combined.

To bake: Preheat the oven to 325°F. Gently pour the filling into the prebaked crust. Bake in the oven for 30 to 35 minutes, until there is little to no jiggle in the center of the pan when agitated.

Let cool completely before slicing. Cut into 24 even bars. The bars can be stored, covered, in the refrigerator for up to 1 week.

Earl Grey Chai Blend

I am a chai aficionado, and I do not say that lightly. I have tried at least fifty different chais in my life, and I am very picky. But the word "chai" means different things to different people. In Hindi, chai translates to "tea," both the leaves and the drink. During my travels in Turkey, the chai we were served was often just a cup of simple black tea. But in America and in other parts of the world, we've come to associate the word "chai" with the masala-style chai, a deeply spiced tea drink that's often sweetened and mixed with milk. My Earl Grey chai is reminiscent of this version and is just as complex, but instead of a mixture of spices, it melds four different floral elements: the stringent lavender, the heady bergamot, the sweet Tahitian vanilla, and the sharp floral aroma of honey. The different tones all play together and then are offset by the tannins of the black tea and the creaminess of the oat milk for a lushly nuanced drink. This recipe was added to the book at the behest of Bavel staff, who flood my kitchen hoping to score a cup whenever I make it.

MAKES 9 CUPS

4 cups water

¼ Tahitian vanilla bean, seeds scraped and pod reserved (may substitute 1 whole Madagascar bean)

¼ cup loose-leaf Earl Grey tea

4 teaspoons dried or fresh lavender leaves and flowers

4 cups oat milk

⅓ cup wildflower honey, or to taste (may substitute any honey)

In a large saucepan over high heat, add the water and vanilla bean seeds and pod. Bring to a boil. Add the tea and lavender and decrease the temperature to a simmer. Simmer over low heat for 3 to 5 minutes, depending on the strength of tea desired (the longer it simmers, the stronger the tea). Add the milk and increase the heat to medium. Heat until you reach your preferred drinking temperature; do not let the milk boil. Remove the pan from the heat and stir in the honey until it has dissolved. Strain through a fine-mesh sieve and serve immediately or store in an airtight container in the refrigerator for up to 5 days. The tea can be served cold over ice or gently reheated in a saucepan over medium-low heat until steaming.

Pomegranate-Hibiscus Sorbet

Pomegranates are very emblematic of the Middle East. Whenever I go with Ori to Israel in late summer or early fall, I love getting freshly squeezed pomegranate juice from one of the little fruit stands throughout the city, or first thing in the morning when Ori's dad makes it for me in his crazy industrial-strength juicer. This sorbet is indicative of our entire restaurant, a cross between the Middle Eastern pomegranate with a nod to the Hispanic culture of L.A. through the hibiscus (jamaica). Hibiscus has a tart, berrylike flavor similar to pomegranate, and we always have some on hand to brew a batch of jamaica agua fresca for the family meal. I find this sorbet super refreshing by itself, but it's also delicious paired with a chewy ginger cookie and candied Concord grapes, or as a slushy granita (see Variation).

MAKES 1 QUART

SPECIAL EQUIPMENT:

Ice cream maker

⅓ cup (10g) loosely packed dried hibiscus flowers

2¼ cups boiling water

1 cup granulated sugar, plus more to taste

2 cups fresh pomegranate juice (may substitute store-bought juice)

1 tablespoon freshly squeezed lemon or lime juice

1 tablespoon vodka

Pinch of kosher salt

In a medium bowl, steep the hibiscus flowers in the water for 5 minutes. Strain through a fine-mesh sieve and reserve 2 cups of the tea.

In a large saucepan, mix the 2 cups tea and the sugar. If any sugar crystals are still visible and undissolved, cook slowly over low heat until the sugar has completely dissolved. Remove the pan from the heat and let cool.

Once cooled to room temperature, stir in the pomegranate juice, citrus juice, vodka, and salt. Taste to determine whether it needs more sugar. If so, add up to 2 tablespoons more to taste.

Pour the mixture into a bowl, cover with plastic wrap, and refrigerate until completely chilled, at least 4 hours or up to overnight. Transfer the mixture to an ice cream maker and churn according to the manufacturer's instructions. Store in an airtight container in the freezer for up to 1 week. Serve in small bowls or coupes.

Variation: To make a granita, pour the unchurned mixture directly into a cake pan or casserole dish and freeze. When ready to serve, remove from the freezer and rake the amount of the mixture that you want to serve with a fork. Serve immediately.

Pine Nut Torte with Orange Cream & Coffee

Pine nuts are the star of many Middle Eastern desserts, and I love the way their mild butteriness plays off of the butter flavor in this rich Breton-style torte scented with orange blossom water. We serve it sliced over a pool of refreshing orange cream and a dusting of bitter and aromatic finely ground coffee.

SERVES 10 TO 12

SPECIAL
EQUIPMENT:

*11-inch
springform pan*

1¾ cups (250g) pine nuts

1¼ cups (250g) granulated sugar

1¼ cups (250g) butter, at room temperature, plus more for greasing the pan

2 tablespoons orange blossom water

6 egg yolks, at room temperature, beaten

1 teaspoon kosher salt

⅔ cup (76g) all-purpose flour

⅔ cup (76g) whole-wheat pastry flour

1 teaspoon water

Orange Cream (page 289) for garnish

Freshly fine-ground coffee for garnish

Butter an 11-inch springform pan.

Add the pine nuts and half of the sugar to a food processor and pulse to combine, about thirty quick pulses.

In a stand mixer fitted with the paddle attachment, cream the butter and the remaining sugar on medium-high speed until fluffy, about 5 minutes. Add the orange blossom water and mix on medium speed until combined. Then add the pine nut–sugar mix and continue to cream on medium speed for about 2 minutes. While mixing, add all but 1 tablespoon of the egg yolks, a little bit at a time, until combined.

In a medium bowl, add the salt and all-purpose and pastry flours and whisk to combine.

With the mixer on low, slowly add the flour mixture to the butter mixture and mix until just combined.

Pour the batter into the prepared pan and spread evenly. Chill, uncovered, in the refrigerator for at least 1 hour. Alternatively, cover the torte with plastic wrap directly touching the surface and chill for up to 2 days before baking.

When ready to bake, preheat the oven to 350°F. Add the water to the reserved egg yolk. Brush the egg wash over the top of the torte with a pastry brush. Score the top of the torte with a knife in a crosshatched pattern.

Place the springform pan on a sheet pan. Bake for 55 minutes, until deep golden-brown. Let cool for at least 2 hours before serving. If making in advance, the completely cooled torte can be fully wrapped in plastic wrap and stored at room temperature for up to 1 day.

To plate each serving, spoon 2 to 3 tablespoons of the orange cream onto a plate. Top with a slice of the torte and dust the top with sifted ground coffee for garnish.

CONTINUED

Orange Cream

MAKES ABOUT 2¼ CUPS

1½ cups heavy whipping cream
½ cup whole milk
⅓ cup granulated sugar
⅛ teaspoon kosher salt
Zest of 2 oranges
5 egg yolks
½ cup freshly squeezed orange juice, reduced by half
Pinch of citric acid
1½ teaspoons orange liqueur*

Our preferred brand of orange liqueur is Royal Combier.

In a medium saucepan over medium-low heat, combine the cream, milk, sugar, salt, and orange zest and heat until scalding and the sugar has dissolved, about 12 minutes.

In a small bowl, whisk the egg yolks. Slowly add half of the hot cream mixture to the yolks while whisking to temper. Pour the egg mixture back into the pan and cook over medium-low heat, whisking continuously, until thickened, about 4 minutes.

Fill a large bowl with ice and nest a medium bowl in the ice. Strain the mixture through a fine-mesh strainer or chinois into the medium bowl to chill. Then add the reduced orange juice, citric acid, and liqueur and stir to combine. Store the cream in an airtight container in the refrigerator for up to 5 days.

About the Authors

Ori Menashe and Genevieve Gergis are the chef-owners of Bestia and Bavel restaurants in Los Angeles. They live in the hills of Silver Lake with their daughter Saffron (yes, named for the spice), and their dog Caputo, (yes, named for the flour).

Lesley Suter is a two-time James Beard Award–winning editor and writer based in Los Angeles.

Acknowledgments

Special thanks to Christina Raptis, Melissa Lopez, Daniela Mercado, Mikey Priore, Diego Argoti, Mike Glick, Nicole Tourtelot, all our staff at Bavel and Bestia, both past and present, our families and especially our daughter, Saffron, who is our most precious gift.

Index

Published in the United States by Ten Speed Press, an imprint
of Random House, a division of Penguin Random House LLC, New York.
www.tenspeed.com

Ten Speed Press and the Ten Speed Press colophon are registered
trademarks of Penguin Random House LLC.

Library of Congress Cataloging-in-Publication Data
Names: Menashe, Ori, author. | Gergis, Genevieve, author.
Title: Bavel : modern recipes inspired by the Middle East / Ori Menashe and Genevieve Gergis.
Description: First edition. | Emeryville : Ten Speed Press, 2021.
Identifiers: LCCN 2020027867 (print) | LCCN 2020027868 (ebook) | ISBN 9780399580932 (ebook) |
    ISBN 9780399580925 (hardcover)
Subjects: LCSH: Cooking, Middle Eastern. | LCGFT: Cookbooks.
Classification: LCC TX725.E35 (ebook) | LCC TX725.E35 M46 2021 (print) | DDC 641.5956—dc23
LC record available at https://lccn.loc.gov/2020027867
LC record available at https://lccn.loc.gov/2020027868

Hardcover ISBN: 978-0-399-58092-5
eBook ISBN: 978-0-399-58093-2

Printed in China

Editor: Emma Rudolph
Designer: Emma Campion | Production designers: Mari Gill and Mara Gendell
Production manager: Serena Sigona
Prepress color manager: Jane Chinn
Prop stylist: Joni Noe
Copyeditor: Dolores York | Proofreader: Sharon Silva | Indexer: Ken DellaPenta

10 9 8 7 6 5 4 3 2 1

First Edition